CW00541463

"... Kent Johnson has taken up arms in a seemingly
that of the 'post-avant' poetry scene. In this thea
scalpel to the formation of our ideological consci⟨
ters more and more as it maps, investigates, and i
where we are."—Ammiel Alcalay

"These poems, at times brutal or pornographic, mourn the ambiguous lega-
cies of an empire now in crisis [. . .] If, in Johnson's work, poetry must change
itself by taking that long hard look in the mirror, what shows is no merely blithe
or tortured or self-referential celebration of the writing act, but an unflinching
courage that demands to know how each one of us . . . is implicated in violence.
Tellingly, Johnson resurrects what are in fact quite ancient formal and stylistic
modes for these contemporary transgressions; his is not an *avant* that engineers
a *tabula rasa* but one that looks back to the memory of our (human) race, where,
as he suggests, translation comes before poetry and not the other way around."
—Vivek Narayanan

"Like the Jews, if Kent Johnson didn't exist, someone would have to invent him.
His mind leaks nomads constantly naming world-historic hinges as if inscrip-
tion were always underfoot. You can't pull Catullus out of the 'incubated / god,
writing himself into being' but you can pull the door open. Literature is close to
fraud, evanescent and trembling in these times of incipient terror. Johnson's ap-
proach deconstructs and exacerbates that fraud; I think of his work as returning
to the (re)creation of language—political and sexual language, the languages of
the last people speaking on earth." —Alan Sondheim

"Lyrical, taut, amused, seeing, pissed. Kent Johnson's poems make me uncom-
fortable. And uncomfortable in a good way."—Hoa Nguyen

Among the poems gathered here I have found insults to my mother's virtue first
scrawled by my father on a brick he hurled through the window of our maid's
bedroom one night in 1977. This happened in Lima, a city with the weather of
London and the body of Los Angeles. The glass shattering is my first memory.
I was never allowed to read the brick. Was Kent Johnson our maid? I can see
him between loads of laundry taking a whiff of my dirty poems and your dirty
poems. Now with his new book against my breast I am pulled to the broken
window and the night mist and bus exhaust and the next thirty years that will
happen to all of us."—Farid Matuk

"The blurbs are over—as hors d'œuvres. It is a question, now, of penultimate
homage to the home age's garden and of non ironic misquotation on the border
of (American) poetry; Kent Johnson writes on such an unparalleled front/ier.
También."—Andrés Ajens

Also by Kent Johnson:

Poetry

Waves of Drifting Snow
Joyous Young Pines
The Miseries of Poetry: Traductions from the Greek (reprinted, UK)
Dear Lacan: An Analysis in Correspondence (reprinted, UK)
Epigramititis: 118 Living American Poets
Lyric Poetry after Auschwitz: Eleven Submissions to the War
He Pearls That We (UK)
I Once Met
Traduciendo a Saenz y otros poemas (Chile)
Lirska poezija nakon Auschwitza (Bosnia-Herzegovina)
Poesía lírica después de Auschwitz (Peru / Spain)

Translations

A Nation of Poets: Writings from the Poetry Workshops of Nicaragua
Have You Seen a Red Curtain in My Weary Chamber?
                                    Writings of Tomás Borge Martínez
Immanent Visitor: Selected Poems of Jaime Saenz
The Night (Jaime Saenz)

Edited Collections

Beneath a Single Moon: Buddhism in Contemporary American Poetry
Third Wave: The New Russian Poetry
Doubled Flowering: From the Notebooks of Araki Yasusada
Also, with My Throat, I Shall Swallow Ten Thousand Swords:
                    Araki Yasusada's Letters in English

Criticism

Poetic Architecture: Twelve Quizzes for a Conceptual Poetry Symposium
Intravistas (forthcoming)
Corroded by Symbolysme: A Critical Mystery (forthcoming)

KENT JOHNSON

Homage
to the Last Avant-Garde

Shearsman Books
Exeter

Published in the United Kingdom in 2008 by
Shearsman Books Ltd
58 Velwell Road
Exeter EX4 4LD

ISBN 978-1-905700-95-0

Acknowledgements

71(+) for GB: An Anthology for George Bowering (Coach House Press, Canada), *A Chide's
Alphabet, Almost Island* (India), *Antennae, Aporia* (Canada), *Backwards City Review,
BathHouse, Big Bridge, BlazeVOX, Bridge, Cambridge Conference of Contemporary Poetry
Translation Series* (UK), *The Canary, Carve, Chicago Review, Circulars, Comunicare*
(Italy), *Coyote* (Brazil), *Damn the Caesars, Dani* (Bosnia), *Does Not Exist, The East Village,
Eating the Pure Light: Homage to Thomas McGrath* (Backwoods Press), *Effing Magazine,
Epigramititis: 118 Living American Poets (BlazeVOX Books), Fascicle, Full Metal Poem*
(Netherlands / Germany), *GAMMM* (Italy), *GutCult, He Pearls that We* (Bad Press, UK),
House Organ, I Once Met (Longhouse Books), *Intemperie* (Chile), *Jacket, La Mariposa
Mundial* (Bolivia), *LA Poetix, La Siega* (Spain), *Lirska poezija nakon Auschwitza* (Ajfelov
Most, Bosnia), *Lyric Poetry after Auschwitz: Eleven Submissions to the War* (Effing Press),
Mandorla, Mano Falsa (Peru), *Mar con Soroche* (Bolivia / Chile), *The Miseries of Poetry:
Traductions from the Greek* (Skanky Possum Press), *Monthly Review, MiPoesias, No: a
journal of the arts, Oasia Broadside Series, Ocho, Octopus, Onedit* (UK), *Origin, Poesía
Lírica después de Auschwitz* (Ediciones Control Quirográfico, Peru / Spain), *Poetry
Project Newsletter, Poets Against The War* (Nation Books), *The Poet's Corner, PP/FF: An
Anthology* (Stacherone Books), *Poezija* (Croatia), *Skanky Possum, Takuapu* (Paraguay),
*The Spoon River Quarterly, Ten Significant American Poets (Azduzbina Kocic Press, Bosnia),
Traduciendo a Saenz y Otros Poemas* (Intemperie Ediciones, Chile), *Tsé-Tsé* (Argentina),
Typo, VeRT, Wherever We Put Our Hats.

Warm thanks are extended to the editors of these magazines and presses.
Thanks are also due to The Cambridge Conference of Contemporary Poetry (UK),
Encuentro Internacional de Poesía Cerros de Oro de Andacollo (Chile), Fundación
Cultural César Patino (Bolivia), Highland Community College, The Illinois Arts
Council, The Illinois Community College Board of Trustees, The National Endow-
ment for the Arts, PEN, and Sarajevo Poetry Days (Bosnia), for generous support
that gave encouragement to the making of a number of these texts.

Contents

For D., B., and A.

You just go on your nerve.

—Frank O'Hara

EIGHT ODES FOR *THE EVERGREEN REVIEW*

KENNETH KOCH

Thanks to his poem about a garbage can
lid being smashed into a likeness of King
George the Third's face, my sixteen year old
son is now writing poetry. This activity has
recently led him into drinking alcohol and
experimenting with drugs, which makes
it difficult for me to say, but I'll say it
anyway: Thank you, Kenneth Koch,
for your marvelous contributions to Poetry.

The following poem represents the first instance of a new poetic form. I have christened it the "Mandrake" (the name used for the mayapple [Podophyllum peltatum] by various 16th and 17th century English poets). Those who would attempt the form in the future must adhere to the following guidelines:

The first, third, fifth, seventh, ninth, eleventh, and thirteenth stanzas (all of them as a group called the "flower") must make some kind of reference to one or two poets of a preceding poetic generation; all of the poets referred to in each of the flower stanzas must have been contemporaries of one another. The stanzas may be written in any meter, rhymed or unrhymed, and may be of any length (prose poetry is also acceptable, as this first example makes clear), but each stanza in the flower must exhibit some sense of parallelism in theme and syntactic logic to its companion flower stanzas.

The second, fourth, sixth, eighth, tenth, twelfth, and final fourteenth stanzas (all of them as a group called the "fruit") must be rendered in prose, with a majority of these stanzas constituting quoted material. There are no other guidelines for the fruit, save that the fruit as a whole be totally dissimilar in theme(s) and tone from the flower, and that the final fourteenth stanza have some reference to the mayapple's seasonal companion, the morel mushroom (in any of the morchella species).

Finally, any "Mandrake" must be led off by some kind of brief introduction, as this originating example is (i.e., the one you are reading right now), so as to provide the poem with a kind of critical or anecdotal stem, a little bit of hollow "normal discourse" propping up the contrapuntal dissonances of theme and tone which the prosodic grid outlined above will inevitably proffer.

★ ★ ★

The New York School (or: I Grew Ever More Intense)

I turned over the bottle of shampoo and Frank O'Hara came out. I rubbed him all into my head, letting the foam rise, knowing I was just warming myself up, excited by the excess of what was to come. Soon, I began to make noisy climax sounds. The scent of oranges and oil paint from a general store in the outlaw town of Shishido (with all its exotic wares) filled the stormy air.

I couldn't help it, I thought of this: *One day, a fortnight or so after my mother's death in Shishido, I was up in the hills playing with some friends. Suddenly one of them said, Look, the baby's hands are all swollen. I touched the baby, which was still strapped to my back, and screamed—it was stone cold. My friends began to panic and jump up and down, shouting, It's dead, it's dead. It felt awful having something dead tied to me, so I ripped off my jacket and dropped the baby, before joining the others as they ran back down the hill as fast as their legs would take them, shrieking.*

I grew ever more intense. I pressed the button on the shaving cream and Barbara Guest came out. I smoothed her taut-as-a-canvass-body all over my cheeks and neck and chin and then I made some hills and valleys in her flatness, using my fingers in an artistic way. The complex smell of dark woods outside the Kamakura town of Hokaisu after a sudden shower (including the eastern smells of sake, persimmon, cicada, cherry blossom, fugu, and haiku) filled the humid air.

I couldn't help it, I thought of this: *Accounts of the horror in the town of Hokaisu have the quality of Hieronymus Bosch's grotesque tableaux of apocalypse: torched villages; macheted babies in the streets; stoned child warriors indulging in cannibalism and draping themselves with the entrails of their victims; peacekeepers—mostly Uruguayans—using their guns only to drive off waves of frantic civilians seeking refuge in their already overflowing compound; a quarter of a million people in frenzied flight from their homes . . . Hundreds of thousands of Congolese have been killed in the fighting, and many more have died as a consequence of the displacement, disease, and hunger that attend it.*

I grew ever more intense. I turned over the aftershave and Ted Berrigan came out. I slapped him just as he was, all pudgy with things, on my face, and he stung, and I yelled at him. I liked it, so I slapped him on me again, hard, and again, yet, then thrice more, and I yelled without restraint. The complex scent of medieval Kyoto filled the heavy air, and there were great wooden and paper prefectures and lots of people with feelings and fears and things like that, just running around like ants, they were, and many kimonoed poets also, their faces lit weirdly by ancient electric screens, competing for cultural capital in a big interactive board game with manifold levels, like in Go, and the stakes were high, very high, for Volvo driving academics died for lack of what was found there.

I couldn't help it. I thought of this: *I was so surprised to see the dark sky over New York with all the red flames through the window because it was only a few minutes before when the sky was blue and clear. It was all quiet and the city was wrapped, enveloped in red flames. Mr. Wakita came to help me. He asked me if I wanted to swim across the river. The bridge was burning and the river was very high. I had no choice. I could barely see by then, though. And Mr. Wakita took my arms and told me to swim across the river together with him, so together we went into the river and began to swim. Swim, you blistered dead baby, swim, he cried, though why he chose these words, I do not know. When we reached the middle of the river, I could no longer see anything and I was starting to feel faint. And as I began to feel faint, I also began to lose control. Mr. Wakita encouraged me and helped me to reach the other side of the river. Finally, we reached the other side. What surprised me so much was all the cries of the students for help and for their mothers. It just didn't stop. I couldn't see anything. All I could do was listen to their cries. I asked my teacher, I asked him what was going on. Mr. Wakita explained to me how the high school students were burnt and crouching in pain in the streets, many of them urinating and defecating openly. I couldn't see anything . . . Some called for help in vain, and some jumped into the river and drowned to death. If my teacher, Mr. Wakita, had not come to help me, I would have died in the Hudson River.*

I grew ever more intense. I squeezed the toothpaste tube and James Schuyler came out. I scrubbed him with my brush against my teeth, looking at myself in the mirror and him all white in my mouth. He tasted like old apricots or hot-house nasturtiums. I spit him out, and the smell of the futuristic city of Pyongyang, when the red calia flower (which symbolizes the Four Eternal Qualities of the Great Leader) is in bloom in all the places of that magical city, where everyone feels gratitude and joy, even though, advanced as these comrades are, they still harbor the prejudices that this poem is not as good as it would be if it had been published in print, in one of the clubby Pyongyang venues of the day, like, say, *Fuck You: a journal of the arts.*

I couldn't help it, I thought of this: *The fourteen young soldiers of the Al-Quram Division, all of them descendants of the NSA-created Royal Court of Pyongyang, mummified by the dry heat but otherwise intact, were found in their sand bunker, crouched and huddled, fetus-like, in a corner, their hands pressed to their ears, their mouths wide open, lips pulled back over their teeth, each in near identical pose and position. Blood from their mouths, ears, noses, urethras, and rectums was caked thickly to their uniforms and bodies. They had been killed by the cumulative force of the Daisy Cutter concussions.*

I grew ever more intense. I turned the button on the deodorant stick and Joseph Ceravolo came out. I slid his bald head back and forth under my arms and began to sing a romantic lied by Harry Partch as arranged by Pauline Oliveros. The aroma of an oil refinery in the twelfth century town of Ishido filled the air, and beneath its huge candled fires, tail-finned cars moved silently in a long slow line, and homeless people, expelled from their lands by the evil Lord of the School of Quietude, with only wooden shingles to cover their private parts, lay motionless under rows of ultra-violet lamps, their necks bizarrely contorted until buds of brown buds sprouted all over their fluorescent bodies, and these, after a time, caught fire as if of themselves; thus, the homeless people perished in this way, giving off the most theatrical screams. They almost sounded like people on fire, jumping from great, towered heights far away in the future, kicking their flame-licked legs the whole way down, you know what I mean, don't you, David Shapiro, you with your spine full of elms, each elm full of little wrens, each wren making a song of green and mauve weather in the elms in your spine, but wait, that's not possible, how could a person have a bunch of singing birds in his spine, oh shut up Joe LeSueur, you pretty geisha boy, end of stanza.

I couldn't help it, I thought of this: *Mr. Giap and his buddies, all illegal immigrants from the town of Ishido, had eaten some rare fresh meat that had suddenly become available in the local market in Saigon one day in 1969, he recalled. Then the U.S. military police came around asking whether anyone had bought that meat in the market. Some American soldiers who were hungry and full of drugs had raped and killed the boy and cooked some of his meat with a flame thrower and eaten it and then sold the rest to the local merchant, and we bought it from that merchant, Mr. Giap said. He added that he had heard that the American soldiers had been punished for the killing and the cannibalism, and that one of them was widely known throughout the U.S. military in Vietnam as an experimental poet of the highest order. This just goes to show you, said Mr. Giap, tersely, that avant-garde poets can appear anywhere and sometimes be very, very bad people. Later that day, Mr. Giap flew to a secret location to address an emergency meeting of the 19th Sector NLF Urban Command.*

I grew ever more intense. I turned over the mouthwash and Kenneth Koch came out. I swished him around and gargled him, making the sound of a drowning Prince in the false 18th century Kingdom of Formosa (the name given to Japan by the infamous forger George Psalmanazar). He (Koch) tasted of secrets and codes, of pre-Socratic papyrus and pussy willow, of communion wafers and coleslaw. The smell of baseball, synesthesia, and Ron Padgett's funny tiny feet bound in purple silk spun by worms grown in trailer truck laboratories furnished by U.S. government Programs for the Arts made an overdetermined smell like (for these are the smells which the pleasures of peace provide) the smell I smelled in Leningrad in 1989, when, wedged between Barrett Watten and Ron Silliman, I entered the closet-sized cloister of a Shinto temple to look at the mummified middle finger of the Russian saint Nishiwaki Junzaburo under glass. We looked at each other sidelong, like fish, each hatching our private plots, pretending we weren't looking at the other.

I couldn't help it, I thought of this: *In the Kingdom of false Formosa, a young girl, perhaps eight or nine years old, climbed out of the burning car in which her mother, father, and sister sat dead, their open-eyed bodies on slow fire. In shock, she walked around in tight circles, her fingers hanging by nerves and skin from her hands. She did not cry or say anything. She simply walked in circles for about five minutes, an impassive look on her face, until she slowly knelt and curled up in apparent sleep on the street, the shooting continuing above her body for another twenty minutes or so. During that time, she bled to death.*

I grew ever more intense. In an outhouse on the hills of Nokaido, I wiped myself and then I went to the sink and depressed the pump on the hand soap dispenser and John Ashbery came out. I scrubbed his essence into my hands and began talking to myself in tongues. Because I was stimulated I pressed out some more of him, and rubbed him all over my calves and thighs, making some hoarse shouts. The fragrance of small birds and large flying machines fabricated of paper and piano wire filled the damp air; the machines were flying from Paris to New York, but the birds, it appeared, were migrating in the opposite way.

I couldn't help it, I thought of this: *I went morel hunting with my son the other day on the hills of Nokaido, his last spring before he leaves for university, he once swathed and strapped to my back, his life now completely other and superior to mine, his handsome looks, his clear mind, his at-ease-in-his-skin mien. And at the top of the hill we found about three pounds of beautiful big mushrooms. Looking at him walking in the woods, hearing him shout out that here's another one, oh, look, father, here's another one, me looking at him, thinking the most sentimental things and shielding my tears from his view: How is it possible the years have gone by like they have and that I will never get them back? How is it that this world is so full of suffering and hurt? I guess when you think about it, I thought, rubbing my drippy nose with my silk sleeve, the left sleeve, where the baby snow crane is raising his wings against the half-moon, well, I guess I've been pretty lucky after all, enjoying the pleasures of calligraphy and sake in all the surplus time the labor of others has more or less made for me. Some of us are like rain, and others of us are like the thirsty ground, and others of us are like parasitical mushrooms, especially poets, and that's just the way things have come to be. The truth is that I felt like running back down the hill as fast as my legs would take me, shrieking, seeking I do not know what. But I gathered my composure and turning toward him said, in deep fatherly voice, Ah, that is wonderful son! The gods of the forest are smiling upon us today.*

WITTGENSTEIN (OR: THOSE WERE THE DAYS)

*Thought is surrounded by a halo. All of a sudden, someone paints a picture in order to
show how he imagines a theater scene!*
                                   —Ron Padgett

It was spring—Primaverus mysteriumus!

Down at *The Eagle* we took turns making him fly
around the room. (Russell and Keynes were already KO'd
in the loo.) Then, one of us hung him up by the back of his
gown against the board. And then another of us cooed, like a boy
playing a girl, "for thus sings he; Cuckoo. Cuckoo." And then
we had some shots and some stout, and spoke like men do. And then
we took out our dart cases (lacquered and dark, like the compacts
of sluts) and aimed. We aimed inside the rules of the game that is named:
"Why Is There Somethinge Rather Than Nothinge?"

O Pembroke, with your portrait of Spenser and your Chris Smart Room!

O Christ's, with your portrait of Marlowe, the pederast and spy!

O King's, with your massive green and your flowers and punts and your
red-hot poker with which the insufferable prick threatened our Popper!

Poetry Blogs (of the Fourth Generation) in Zürich

I was having dinner with Francis Picabia, Kurt Schwitters, and the Count of Lautréamont. Some other minor poets of the pre-war years were there. A slave boy from the Spanish colonies loyally fanned the room. Lautréamont was dead, of course, and his boiled body was being served in thin slices stuffed into baguettes the shape of small pods which characterize the genus *Asclepias*.* Everything was going famously: Picabia was making Vvvvvv sounds, holding the severed wheel of his crashed Belogna; Ball was flapping his papier-maché wings at top velocity; and Man Ray's three mistresses, with their pointed, penitent hoods, were sipping absinthe and whispering mysteriously near the lime tree. Then it happened that Breton gave his ten year old, bowl-cutted son, Aragon (a clique-herding brat affecting the most pompous equanimity), a slice of the Count's perfectly shaped derrière. The child swallowed and immediately commenced to gag and retch, his little hands going to his throat, like the hands of a shot head of state, and he turned violet throughout the whole area of his slightly pudgy body. Nadja began to ululate, and Breton began to blurt primal commands, his shouts seeming to come from elsewhere, as if the hand of some Other were up his spine. The sounds coming from the child were those of crows, or something else I cannot yet name. In this moment of crisis, I did not choke, nosiree, I did not: I sprinted over and performed the maneuver I had brought with me from the future, the *Heimlich*, as it is known, wrapping my arms around the bug-eyed munchkin, squeezing and lifting his rib cage with all my might in five rapid thrusts. It worked! There on the parquet floor, writhing, covered in a film of slime, was a baby shark. "How on earth did *that* get into him?" cried Lacan, in his ballooned pantaloons. "I don't know, but I could give a shit," growled Gertrude Stein. "Pass the butter."

* *i.e., Milkweed*

POEM UPON A TYPO FOUND IN AN INTERVIEW OF KENNETH KOCH, CONDUCTED BY DAVID SHAPIRO[1]

1. First of ill, I fell in love.

2. I could, of course, go on and on.

3. The gapeseed trees leaned down; the humors of a flying thing broke swith in a deafening whoosh.

4. Well, certes, this just shows our tholen souls have been braided everywhen as one.

5. And therefrom, the sun shone down thro the missled hole upon the praying ones and.

6. It was full of smoke in that dome, fore the days of no smoking.

7. I remember those good old days, whilom it was me, and Will and Ben and Chris and the wholesome lads of the laste avant-garde.

8. And always, eke, that tother, the girl whose number was a misterium to me.

9. She blew out some rings and did say: It seems I am losing my trellis of thought, rushing with you through this tunnel of trees, whitherward our fate we canst know, nor whencesoever we have come, nor usward what speeds.

10. For there are coins where once there were our eyne.

11. I liked the little hussy that way, naked but for a brassiere, how she could say the darndest things and with such casual mien, as if a kind of chord falling from her spine were plugged into some vast background dump of language.

12. (Exaltingly, eftsoons, I sawed her in the sweven of the flowering trees. She was a plane girl, really, ilke, fain and yare, with wings all swoopstake on her thorax plus eyne of tinsel shillings. Stilled, I lived her with all my might, chasing a horse amain into the sun. You'd never know it now from my face. It was more archaic than it now seems, was more like the sun. Stained and morning-breathéd, we woke in Atocha, to puissant concussions alow the ground.)[2]

13 (a). My nickname at Christ's College was "Beuys"; I spent five years in its crucified sanatorium, whence, a foil upon my temples, great voltage did floode my soiled bodie.

13 (b). But, anyway, to continue and for exemplars: Please observe how in this amber light the prints of the figs are perfectly preserved and.

14. Not to mention that the one whose name is Love is in the form of a faucet.

15. And should it seem at the end of every verse that I am washing my hands of the people and cranes whom I have hammered into this foil for fun, well, then that is the way of the silly sun.

16. Lit from within, as if the fractures in the loveliness were intentionally stressed to the point where it all might just come apart, but not yet qwuite.

17. Peradventure, as if to illustrate, the giant exchange student from the colonies entered the foiled room.

18 (a). Roman and ebonied, eyes whited by the burn, he cried forth and broke the spell:

18 (b). How come is a bus in a desert on fire, he did say, gardyloo.[3]

19. Prithee, thee, quickly, now, break thro this water! (unidentified female voice in the room)

20. For don't you know, dude (the giant continued), that's what your hair will be: Flames shooting upward until you wouldn't see because it were so high up there.

21. I know it sound incredible, somedeal, OK?

22. And I know you be sad and happy at a great flip-flop velocity.

23. But I shit you not: Stop clapping, hug your kin, and look immediately to the sky.

[1] In 1972, in the library of Pewaukee High School, in Pewaukee, Wisconsin, I opened, for no particular reason, a copy of *Poetry* magazine, ca. late 60's, in which happened to be featured David Shapiro's 'Poems from Deal.' I was 16, and I read there that Shapiro had composed the poems when he was 18. I had never read poetry like this before (I'd read little poetry, period), and I mark that encounter as what "turned me on" to poetry, thus changing my life. (Whether I should thank Shapiro with all of my heart or send him a very powerful letter bomb is a question I often ask myself.)

[2] For what the coincidence is worth, this poem was published at *Jacket* Magazine the day before the Atocha Station train bombings in Spain. *Jacket*'s esteemed editor, John Tranter, can verify this odd detail.

[3] Translation, in all instances, approved by The U.S. Treasury Department's Office of Foreign Assets Control.

I Remember Once, Years Ago

I remember once, years ago, before the War that is with us, just after I
had joined the Poetics List, George Bowering sent in a post that said
[I think I remember it rightly], "I am sitting here. The girls have just
gone out for juice and cigarettes." Lots of things happened on the
Poetics List after that, but for some reason I always remembered that
post. I also remember that George and David Bromige used to joke
back and forth a lot, you could tell they were old Vancouver pals, and
sometimes Rachel Loden and another woman, whose name on the list
was number thirty, I think, I can't recall, used to chime in, and it was
all pretty clever and erotic, actually, for they would often say things
that seemed quite inappropriate for a public space like Poetics, but you
could tell everyone really liked it and wanted more. I often thought to
myself then: "I wonder what George Bowering looks like?" And whenever
I thought of him, I imagined him sitting there, debonair, smoking a
        cigarette
that one of his women had brought back from the store, typing things
about his lust for Rachel Loden, whom I interviewed once and who
is a terrific poet and who would always naughtily answer George
or David and give them a run for their money. Years later, I was sitting
with David Bromige in Samuel Pepys' rooms at Cambridge, where he
was the guest of honor at a conference of contemporary poetry, and I
looked at David sitting there, very calm, by the leaded glass window
that was open onto the river that flowed under the rooms [he had just
given the most magnificent reading], and I thought to myself, "You
know, I really like this man, I really do, even though we fought a lot
on the Poetics list." And I thought about all the jokes he and George
        Bowering
would make, sometimes at my expense, and how mad that would make me,
o madder than a two-peckered goat, or how they would chatter away
sometimes about how much they were in love with each other, or the jokes
about lingerie or friendly bondage they would make with Rachel and the
woman who was number thirty and how everyone on the list laughed at
that, though secretly all the avant-garde poets were very aroused, and I
thought to myself, "Why, wasn't all that other stuff just rather silly—wasn't
the champion part about it all the good sexy banter, or when George

Bowering used to suddenly get excited, for you could tell that he was
excited, and rhapsodize at the slightest provocation about baseball, all
he needed was the slimmest excuse and sometimes none? I wonder if he
is still like that, you never see him posting much anymore, maybe he gets
free cigarettes as the Poet Governor, or whatever they call the big thing
up there, maybe he doesn't have to imagine sex over email anymore,
      maybe
he gets that free now, too, and for real, Canada being very liberal and all,
like California. I hope the War ends soon. I hope George Bowering is
      happy . . ."
And David Bromige's head was turned now, so that with the light, his face
seemed set in relief into the leaded glass, and he said, "Is it just me, or is
      it a little hot in here?"

Flood, or: I Hope You're OK
[with some phrasing by Nazim Hikmet]

It's devastating. It's got to be doubly devastating on the ground.
> —George W. Bush, flying over New Orleans in Air Force One,
> September 1, 2005.

*New Orleans is more likely to be under the ocean as the result of a
hurricane than eaten by termites . . .*
> —Laura Mullen, in Baton Rouge, e-mail to me, August 10, 2005,
> shortly before Katrina

When the hurricane came, I wrote Laura Mullen, and I said,
I hope you're OK, I hope not too many manuscripts have been
lost, all the records from the War, for example, the letters of
the boys from the front, the super-heated star in their hearts,
their groins aching so, the citizens so frightened, huddling in
attics, pressing their noses to the roofs, looking up, breathing
deep, the water still rising, bloated bodies floating by, all the
paintings and stuff, the letters and the poems, the SUV's bobbing
like urns, the holdings of the US de Vere Society soaked to a pulp,
half the papers of Truman Capote, too, drafts by Arakawa & Gins
for "The Architecture against Death," mush now, the cylinder seals,
the smashed lions with wings, sunk in silt, hundreds of pilgrims
trampled or jumping from a bridge to smash against the levee
below, rumor of a suicide bomber, "a false alarm," start your own
blog or something, say what's on your mind, and can it with the
lame "literary" stunts, the poet said, I hope you're OK, the Earth
spinning in blank space, cold now, not like a block of ice, or a
dead cloud even, but like an empty walnut, the wetlands under

pavement, the President cutting his long vacation by a day,

breathing deep, flying over the flood, nose pressed to the glass,

lots of water, a riot of looters below, the rage rising, the children

looking up, crying, diving for cover, clutching six-packs of

pop, all the bombs to come in their super-heated hearts, you must

grieve for this right now, the poet said, the Earth spinning

in blank space, the call to prayer from the minaret, slaves

huddled in the hold, noses pressed against the hatch, breathing

deep, the water still rising, I hope you're OK, Laura, who knows

what will happen, I hope I can still come to Louisiana to read, I'll

come in a little sailboat if I have to, Guido and Lagia, too, the poet

said, I'm trying to smile in allusions for you, all full of myself,

always bringing it back to myself, I hope we all make it,

wherever we're sailing, I hope there's some kind of reason

for it, all these sails shredding like clouds in a furious wind,

the pilgrims broken like straw on the levee below, though

some are moving there, spreading their hands, like supplicants,

still, calling for their god, the water still rising, I hope you're OK.

PHOTOGRAPH OF EMILY DICKINSON

—for John Wieners

Life, this Sphere — Infinite —
Death enshrouds the Paradox —
Its surround not a vestment,
But the skin of an Aperture,
Pulled — Taut — to an aura of Soul's
Form — confused Heaven —
Lit and ecstasied by you — This book
By my hand. This flower that I hold
In my hand, in the shock of your Life.

Five Sentimental Poems for Angel Hair

I Dreamt Us Having a Pure Father and Son Moment

For dreaming, I saw my son. And the tears fell and fell.
       —Edwin Denby

I dreamt us having a pure father and son moment, you had just
returned from the long Vipassana retreat, and I asked, "What was it
like," and you said, "Look into my eyes," and I did, and there was no
discomfort in the doing of it, it was like looking in a mirror at my
own eyes, and then, at that moment, at one and the same time, tears
fell from your eyes and mine, and they fell and fell, and I said, "What
is it you've seen," and you said, without reflecting, as if you were
me, "I've seen these tears on your lips," and you brushed your thumb
across my lips and then brought it to your own, wet with your own
tears, and then you took my hand and brushed my thumb across your
lips and brought it back to my own, and we kept looking into each
other's eyes without thought for a long time, and this time continued,
gathering up in its transparent sentiment all of our pain, all of what
might have been between us and never was, and there was no fear,
or sadness, or shame, yet there were so many things, they filled the
whole world, and it all swelled in our eyes and fell and fell, and our
looking into each other in this dream, ever rushing toward its end,
never stopped or changed.

"Even though he's known as a Language poet, I want to write like Norman Fischer"

"Even though he's known as a Language poet, I want to write like Norman Fischer," he said to me, out of nowhere, leaving.

For sesshin, "but I probably never will," the mountain.

Towering in the picture behind the boy's head, his little brother's head reaches to his shoulder, trees.

And trees, and a river, far away, disappearing into the younger one.

His hand on his brother's shoulder, he has to reach up a long ways.

To put it there, the sky is blue, though fading now from sun against the picture, there are.

No clouds, but far mountains, and trees, and sky, they are alive, they love each other, they are.

Contented, it is spring, one now is dead, the other sits in sesshin, "Who is.

Alive and who is dead?" the words come from far away, his back.

Is straight as a dead pine on a mountain, still standing in the clear.

Cut, it reaches, towering into the sky, "Who's next?" shouts the monk, it is spring.

SENTIMENTAL PISCATORIAL

The fishing was good this morning, though
we never made it to the Mississippi. The Apple
is a lovely tributary; once I almost drowned [1]

in its green, but that was a long time ago,
and I didn't, because I guess life still
needed something there. Well,

for instance, as I said to my son Brooks,
who is starting to be a poet, many times
(as I've said many times to him, that is), if [2]

you are going to put your life into
poetry, make sure you stay low, walk slow,
and lay the fly right along the velocity

changes. The sun was just starting to burn-
off the fog, and a doe walked across the riffle
right upstream and didn't startle. A heron stood

in the next pool, shimmering, "like
some kind of religious lawn ornament,
when you think about it," my son [3]

said. And so I watched my son fish,
covered in an actual gold, like his
drug-inspired poem of the alcoholic man

with the burning city in his heart. I [4]
watched him fish, trying so to impress me,
his back to the sun. [5]

[1] The first stanza is, perhaps over-obviously, an allusion to John Ashbery's 'Into the Dusk-
Charged Air.'

² The second and third stanzas are prosodic glosses on Frank O'Hara's "Why I Am Not a Painter." Interestingly, the following email response was received from Hilton Kramer, editor of *The New Criterion*, to whom this poem (sans footnotes) was originally submitted: "Dear Mr. Johnson, I like the poem quite a lot; it has an easy and laconic sound breaking elegantly across an unusual and complex meter (the ionic as base foot is idiosyncratic, to say the least, and quite impressive). Still, I am afraid I have to pass this time around—Guy Davenport, who has the last word with all poems submitted to NC, felt that the poaching, as he put it, from O'Hara in the second and third stanzas was too cute and obvious. But I will tell you that Mr. Davenport found the poem's ending "strangely moving," and I can tell you, too, that he doesn't often offer up such words as "moving" in his reports to me. Please do send us more of your poems. —HK"

³ When Brooks was a child, I would read him poems at bedtime. Wallace Stevens (the Stevens of *Harmonium*) and Kenneth Koch were his favorites. I now realize that Brooks would never have said what he did about the heron appearing as a lawn ornament had it not been for Koch's line in that love poem about the parts of speech, where the garbage can lid is smashed into a likeness of the face of King George the Third.

⁴ This is an allusion to St. Augustine's City of God, which is the theme, if you will, of my son's painting. In the upper corner of the canvass, in tiny, calligraphic lettering, my son has written the following passage from Augustine's *Soliloquia*, which he copies from *Doubled Flowering: From the Notebooks of Araki Yasusada*, the heteronymous masterpiece of "Tosa Motokiyu," of whose manuscripts, it is by now widely known, I am one of the caretakers:

> For how could the actor I mentioned be a true tragic actor if he were not willing to be a false Hector, a false Andromache, a false Hercules? Or how could a picture of a horse be a true picture unless it were a false horse? Or an image of a man in a mirror be a true image unless it were a false man? So if the fact that they are false in one respect helps certain things to be true in another respect, why do we fear falseness so much and seek truth as such a great good? Will we not admit that these things make up truth itself, that truth is so to speak put together from them?

⁵ *This is an allusion to an image in a poem by Whitman, where the sun behind a man standing in the water forms a golden aura around him. But I cannot now recall the exact poem.*

POEM FOR AN ANTHOLOGY OF "POEMS OF THE MIND"

We are preparing an extensive anthology (approximately 800 pages) of poetry that explores the nature of "mind itself" in any of the ways that it has been "knowable" through poetry.
     — George Quasha and Charles Stein, eds.

 for my sons, Brooks and Aaron

This is not a poem about the mind, but a poem
about the sky, which thinks its thunderclouds out loud
and its crows and its rain, and then, when becalmed
and asleep, when a moon drifts through, dreams horses,
or hearses, or two figures facing, back-lit and aureoled,
the two figures there standing, in a dhow with a sail

that is already shredding. You can see them coming
slowly into this thinking, a writer and his reader,
each reaching for the other, aware there is nothing
below the sky, reflected where they are sailing,
nothing but each other to hold to, mere figments
of its weathers, which bless with such joy and blast

with such fear, so fickle and weird these weathers!
They are reaching out, in the boat that is dying
into the sky that is dreaming, and then they are gone,
just like that, even as others are appearing to take their
place and to do, as it were, the sky's bidding: minareted
kingdoms rising and falling, and night-goggled warriors

crawling, and burning children with blood spurting,
and bannered towers collapsing, and swept-winged
planes conquering, and many strange forms that have never
been thought and thus have no names: forms always new
and changing. And that's how the sky is, things arising
and things going away, and in a way, we could say, it's

a never to be opened gift we are given by something,

just as we come falling into this dreaming: a sky
reflected where we are sailing, and where we reach out
without reaching the beloved who faces us, and who
also is reaching, while we watch the thoughts come,
and watch the thoughts go.

Unedited Notes toward a Poetic Essay on the Translation of Poetry

What is the translation of poetry, anyway?

I, for one, don't have the foggiest idea.

Do you?

No one knows what Poetry is:

So how could we ever grasp the nature of its shadow?

No, that's already making a claim on it . . . ["its shadow"]

As if Translation came after, when maybe it's Poetry that does . . .

And also, who knows about the Sun?

These past weeks, I've been writing emails to wonderful translators of poetry. [and here they are] [and I'm pleased to say] [and now they are gathered here] [the overwhelming response has been]

I read somewhere that you can tell how fast any sun is moving away from you by reading its "red shift" along a spectrum of light.

These works are spread across a spectrum of light—We call them all "translations," and we are waving, as they grow smaller in the distance, and we grow smaller to them. [explain the "we"]

No doubt this is a bit much for some tastes.

[Benjamin on the Afterlife and royal robes. Spicer on the radio and transmission]

But I've been embroiled in controversies related to translation for many years now, and it's made me somewhat eccentric, I guess.

Suddenly, now, I am forty-nine, and I find I'm as confused as ever!

There is even a warrant out in Greece for my arrest. [stress the charges of murder are false]

But who wants to read some long, narcissistic tale about a translator's personal problems?

My son comes into the room, reading, as he does, *One Hundred Poems from the Chinese*, the duct tape glistening on its spine.

He closes it and lays it down, softly, like a hurt moth, next to the lamp.

What are you doing, he says.

I'm trying to write an essay on the translation of poetry for the first issue of a magazine, I say, tossing back the last of my wine . . .

. . . and I just can't figure out how to bring it to a close. [sigh]

Well, he says, beginning to roll a cigarette, why don't you say this—it will be pretty melodramatic, but so what, the stakes in this are high [pauses to lick cigarette and put between lips] and there's not a whole lot of time, Dad, for euphemism [sound of Zippo clicking open, now shutting]:

"With Translation's gasoline," he says, in his changed voice, smoke issuing from his mouth, "Poetry sets itself on fire, so it might live by the light of its self-immolation."

Wow, I say, that's really good son. It's in! [writing]

Thanks, he says. It's kind of a free translation from Rexroth's version of "Watching It Snow and Thinking of My Friend, the Hermit Hu."

And then he picks his book back up and lets it fall open again, to wherever it mothy might.

I remember it just as it was, the sun through the screen behind him, the coiling smoke, the open book, the profile of his face, the sound of clanging, of someone hammering away, for whatever reason, at iron in the distance . . .

[representing nearly twenty languages and thirty nations] [most all of it in English for the first time] [no translation is intended for any reader, and so forth]

And the distance has grown so great and at such speed.

And he is in the darkness now from me and with such velocity, even the sadness of the space where he once stood, reading, is darkly beautiful for it.

And I can't really say, looking at all these translations before me, what is faithfulness, nor what is so faithful it has flowered, without shame, into falsity.

Twenty Traductions and Some Mystery Prose for *"C": A Journal of Poetry*

PREFATORY NOTE

Alexandra Papaditsas died, under still unsolved circumstances, in her native mountain village of Thylakis, in May, 2002. She was 42. A victim of the rare syndrome *Cornuexcretis phalloides*, wherethrough a large keratinous horn grows from the head, she spent most of her life sheltered in a small Gnostic monastery outside the port city of Patmos.[1] When she courageously returned to live in her village in 1998 (courageous, for her horn approximated the size and shape of a billy goat's), she was shunned, regarded as a witch, and on more than one occasion, stoned by villagers. This was how I met Alexandra, in fact, happening upon her cowered form (this was January, 1999, on my first of three trips to Thylakis) behind a taverna, shortly after a group of teenage boys had assaulted her.

Though it disturbingly reveals the paranoia and mental anguish she suffered in her last days, I have, after deliberation, chosen to publish, without emendations, the introduction she wrote for this gathering. It is clear—frayed and matted to a semantic felt by suffering though they are—that these words were written with intent that they be published alongside our co-translations. I cannot decipher what meaning is attached to the epigraphs she chose from Virgil, Goethe, Lacan, and Dickinson.

There is not much more, frankly, that I wish to explain. Enough hurt and misunderstanding has taken place. Thus, I offer her introduction here, verbatim, even though its wild claims may put me in a suspicious light, no doubt engendering further rumors about my person, as if there weren't enough already. And perhaps, who knows, I deserve any opprobrium that may come my way. Let the gods decide.

In addition, I have let her final bracketed insertions within the poems stand, marks of delirium though they may be. Perhaps in some sense these marks are also mine, her pain having some Archaic source in me, though I barely understand the wherefore. Perhaps, indeed, her textual eruptions should be seen (may the reader forgive me) as bony knobs sprouting from the heads of such minotaurish translations as these-- weird but extrinsic appendages of the ravaged body in which they root, pathetic onyxian projections of love's ultimate excrescence into misprision and sorrow.[2]

In three thousand years, may her curling horn be found within the layered strata of asteroidal debris.

—Kent Johnson

[1.] The monastery is one of the important sites of the Gnostic Order of Greece (Authentic Synod), a small syncretic sect founded in 1874, which centaurishly fuses traditions of ancient Greek paganism with Eastern Orthodox Christian practices. Percy Bysshe Shelley, depicted in church frescoes in Patmos with human torso and goat legs, is one of the sect's saints. The Gnostic Order is most influential in the Northern Aegean, particularly on the islands of Chios, Lesbos, and Samothraki, where it counts with modest but long-standing congregations. It was in the Patmos monastery, in collaboration with a "Brother Kallikteros," that Alexandra labored unsuccessfully for years to crack the code of Linear Script A, an extinct second millennium B.C. language inscribed on scores of clay tablets and fragments that have been excavated around the Mediterranean over the past century. Linear Script B, a later and distantly related archaic Greek dialect, was famously decoded by the epigrapher Michael Ventris in 1952.

[2.] I have also chosen to publish, as an appendix, a letter sent to me by Papaditsas shortly before her death and a letter I received from Father Savvas, Pan-Abbot of the Greek Gnostic Monastery of Patmos, at a later date. I had written him asking for a comment of endorsement to this book. Though his reply was shocking and painful to me, I feel I have no choice but to be forthcoming about it.

INTRODUCTION

But now we are in the cavern. Begin your song.
                    —Virgil

Be bold, bold without rein, and great men and women will come to your aid.
                    —Goethe

Well, when I was a young psychiatrist in Paris, when the City was innocent yet, the man-boy Artaud was a patient under my care. It was a difficult case (imagine treating a patient who has written on the walls in his own shit, "People who come out of nowhere to try to put into words any part of what goes on in their minds are pigs."): In the end, electro-shock was the only way in. He was blue and stiff as a kite in a Chinese wind. "He is LIKE A GOD!" screamed Dali in Spanish, standing behind me, his bony fingers clutching my hips, while Michaux, in turn, clutched those of him clutching mine (we had, the three of us, with our respective disciples, only just that week severed resolutely with the execrable Breton) and were inseperable, like peas in a pod . . . Yes, it was as if he, Artaud, were (oh, his gauze-filled mouth) a kilometer up in the air, attached to a taut and humming string, and we holding fast to him.
                    —Jacques Lacan

You have so far to go in your poetry, and it's going to be hard for you to get there, but maybe you can do it if you try very, very hard. Will you try?
                    —Jim Chapson (spoken to my dear love, Kent Johnson,
                        in Axel's Bar, Milwaukee, Wisconsin, ca. 1978)

Hold fast to me, my whore; let us parasail into the paratext.
                    —Emily Dickinson

I am very happy to at last present these traductions of poems drawn from glorious antiquity. Some of these poems have been translated before, even many times, by scholars whose hands and skulls are luminous with the gold leaf of glory. We (me and the Dead Translator who has ravaged me) have poured now more mystery into them. Beware immediately: Buds of pussy willow will break out under the reader's arms.

Some are traduced in the first time. This has occurred with astonishing thanks to the Montazah Palace find of 1998, where over four hundred philosophical and poetical papyri were discovered, perhaps, I believe, saved from the Alexandria library as it fell burning by Roman hordes. Of course, it is possible also, as he used to say dreamily, his head prepositioned between my lap, that this may be the anachronistic collection of a noblewoman from the Byzantine.

And therefore this book, fragile as a locust screaming its last, it follows such a love affair of the most sandpapered troubles, like a child whose face has been scraped in and out, rawly, in a meat, against the rock, the rough one laid out for me. A man saved a woman so falsely (he saved me on the thistled hilltop, I was driven there by my head-*keras*,[1] the stone throwers kissed their sleepy children goodnight in Thylakis). Then he traitored her, *cracked her four-handled cup* (cipa mezoe tiriowee weke)[2] one would say in phrasing from Linear B—though Mr. Ventris's translation is probably inexact—left her singular on the macadam, by the housing project (Ghettoi). Yes, the situation is ancient, but that doesn't make me feel any better.

Yet it's strange, I am ecstatic at his death, my co-translator, the false one, oh the hole of all his buttocks, which gave me heroin just for traduction favors. I loved him and I hate him, bastard, perambulator, like all my doctors in Patmos, the shockers with dead seas in the eyes (I saw them through my gauze and rubber taste). I loved him and he at one season loved me, his Doric locks. I know it, he bathed my body in rose mallow and honey-thyme, his little goat feet. He grabbed my horn and his eyes went white. Something huge passed overhead. Try . . .

Dionysus!! There was no time: Our bones touched, our Thesauri caught fire by themselves. The priest who married us looked like a giantess with her long beard, his swinging and smoking thing and all the icons, so orthodox around us.[3] The sea lapped into our brains (so erotic!), we greased our bodies and crossed it. Oh, Athena *[Here the pencil has been pressed so hard and insistently in cross-out that there is a darkly haloed four-inch long by two-inch wide hole. KJ]* papyri folded into origami under our thought. "Look, imagine it," he said, fanning himself with an intricate waterfowl, "No one has the foggy West idea what translation is."

And then he departed from me and died, he stepped into a Ferrari, I think, on purpose, in Turin. WHY Hipponax? HOW COME, Anacreon? FOR WHAT Attalyda? POR QUE OR POR QUA Alkaios? HEY Alkman? HUH Kentopholous? WHY Tantalos? His death is a snuff-flick of me. Someone, please, call my mother immediately.

[77] 51-93-03 [4]

Even though I know that poetry is much more than Poetry, I know these are Poems we did in another time, when we were happiest before the terrorist brown color covered everything. I am going to go away now. I am going to go away, like antelopes roaming from Uruguay, where he lived as a boy. The annotations about what is gone in the moths are mine, after his death. I am sure he would disagree. But fuck him, still. Fuck him in the mouth with a great velocity. Minor lying god.

—Alexandra Papaditsas (March, 2002)

[1] *"Keras": The Greek word for horn. KJ*
[2] *Phonetic rendering of phrase from Linear Script B. KJ*
[3] *See the Appendix. KJ*
[4] *Her Mother's phone number in Patmos. I have altered it for obvious reasons. KJ*

Social Dictum

The City is the teacher of Man.

Its cupped, unseen hand

[Here there is an oblong hole, as if burned by laser rays shot out from gauze covered eyes.]

whose shit steams in the public places,
writhes and curls like slugs into letter shapes,
which our slaves, spilling limed water from amphorae,
wash away before the lesson can be read.

—*Xenophanes, ca. 565–473. Poet and historian, resident of Elea. The above work—formerly attributed to Simonides—belongs to his "Silloi" (parodic and satiric hexameters).*

BACCHANALIA OF POETS

[Torn away, as if suddenly thrusting its haunches like an American buffalo.]

pressed into rancid oil for the arses of the discarded,
who rub it on, thinking themselves anointed

[Torn away, as if suddenly offering herself in heat like an American buffalo.]

—*Alkaios, ca. 630-590 B.C. From papyri discovered in 2000 on Lesbos, the poet's home. His poetry, written in Aiolic dialect, is frank and often accusatory. Horace, for one, was greatly impacted by his work.*

On Imitation

Splay the oozing Theophrastus[1] on a catapult.

Pull the pus-covered cart to the Pellaen[2] walls,
and cut the tensed rope.

[Brownish-reddish hole, as if a figure had been rocketed outward.]

Let the assholes of Assus[3] preach about Truth and Form:

In the real world, a philosopher flying over a burning city is
strangely beautiful.

And strange beauty sings that poetry is not bound by imitation.

—*Ammonides, Athenian soldier and poet, friend of Leonidas of Tarentum, he fought in the campaign to liberate Greek cities from Macedonian garrisons following the death of Alexander in 323 B.C. Only three poems by him survive, though scholars have attributed a number of late *Skolia* (anonymous drinking songs) to him.*

[1] Famous student of Aristotle.

[2] The city where Aristotle served as tutor to Alexander.

[3] A reference, in part, to Aristotle, who for three years lived and taught in Assos with Erastus and Xenocrates. Assos was the capital of a small client state ruled by Hermeias, a vassal of the Great King of Persia, and roundly despised by the Athenians.

[The following five poems are by Hipponax. See note at end.]
On the Bastard Boupalous

Be a coatrack for me, dear, while I clock
Boupalous[1] on his snot-filled nose.

Following this, be a four-legged bench,
as I fuck from the rear his sweet,
the idiot giantess of Rhegium.[2]

Thank you, Ibykos, handsome whore-boy,
for supporting my revenge.[3]

[1] Boupalous was a sculptor of Ephesos for whom Hipponax had great enmity. Numerous of Hipponax's poems take him as occasion.

[2] Her name was Arete, and it appears that Hipponax later had a serious amorous relationship with her.

[3] A dig at the court poet Ibykos, famous contemporary of Hipponax.

PROVIDENCE

Not once has the eyeless goddess, Wealth,
come to my hut and said: "Hipponax, I'm
giving you thirty four silver minas and that's
just for starters." Not once.

Slut-Bitch.

CLIFF SWALLOWS DART

[...] cliff swallows dart, as if [...]
[...] place your leg like that [...]
[...] open it as if [...]

[Strange how the thighed absence on either side (eaten by moths) pushes out the ancient sex.]

THE MISERIES OF POETRY

In Lydian tone she said, "Come hither, I will plug up
your tight asshole." And she beat my egg sack with a sprig
of lilac as if I were a satyr. I fell backwards, breathing
heavy, and caught there by writhing vines I suffered
torture times two, and then some: A dried rose stem
lashed my man-tits; someone smeared me with cow's
shit, and then my ass started stinking like Hades.
Dung beetles came, sucked there by the fetid
gook, like roan-filled flies. Bugs with their alphabet-eating
sounds: They covered me and shoved inward, burrowed
deep, filing their teeth without pity on my bones.

I hurt so bad, I might as well have had the Pygelian plague.

On a Serpent Painted on the Aft of a Ship

Mimnes, you sick aesthete! Why'd ya paint a long
snake-thing going up the rear end of our trireme?[1]

We'll be fucked with black luck, become slave-rowers
for pug-nosed Thessalians. We'll get eaten by sea-worms.

Also, our pretty helmsman will grow light-headed from
pressing tight, in fear, the cheeks of his succulent ass.

—*Hipponax, ca. 565-520. Banished from Ephesos, he lived much of his life as a wandering beggar in the nearby city of Klazomenai. He is one of the most demotic, bawdy, and satirically cutting poets of the Lyric Age, almost totally preoccupied with personal topics, and his verse exhibits an earthiness whose imagery often flirts with the fantastic and surreal. As evocatively stated by Herondas in the Palatine Anthology, "O stranger, stay clear of the horrible tomb of Hipponax . . . You might wake the sleeping wasp whose bile would not rest even in Hades, but launches shafts of song in lame measure." Indeed, his meter is unorthodox by Hellenistic standards—Hipponax composed largely in "choliambs," or "lame iambics" with dragging final feet.*

[1] A large galley with three banks of oars.

EROS

On paper wings, pressed by Phokylidos
the Epileptic, I flap to Olympus, panting,
seeking my master, Eros. But he looks
through me, says no more dog-style fucking:
He sees my graying face-hairs and flies off,
looking outwards toward nothing—
while I stand transfixed in the breeze
made by his thin wings of gold.

—*Anakreon, 572–490 BC. With the equally famed Ibykos, he was for many years court poet of Polykrates, the Tyrant of Samos. Upon the murder of his employer, Anakreon moved on to the court of Hippias, Athenian ruler of no less tyrannical nature. His refined and sophisticate verse is almost wholly decadent in theme. He died, it is said, choking on a grape.*

Drums

Drums, sweet and tart,
the thighs thrum

[A hole, as if blown outward with a great force from below.]

You, god who does me,
again and again,

[Again, as if blown outward, greatly, from far below: Like a pool hall, or a bus, or
a restaurant by the sea, or a child, with the rock of David in his hand.]

Eros, raising
the fragrant switch,
who straddles with four legs,
or more.

—Sappho, poet of Lesbos, ca. seventh century B.C. She is, it hardly needs saying, one of
the great lyric voices of any age.

FRAGMENT

[Moths have eaten here. Who sent them?]

they will remember us
by our pieces. Our torsos
will move them to poetry.
They will put our parts on parade,
to imagine what we were,
so to forget what they,
dreaming us, are.

—*Attalyda, provenance and dates unknown. From papyrus discovered in the Montazah Palace find, Alexandria, Egypt, 1998.*

THE SEVEN MUSES OF THE BOAT-MAKING DISTRICT[1]

If I ever see a ghost, I hope it is Brotachos of Alkmena[2].
Because I wouldn't be afraid. I would look at him
Floating there in his lily-shaped bubble, and then I would
Fall asleep and pick up exactly where I'd stopped in
My dream, just as if I'd never left it.

If I ever go to the Cyclades, I hope it is Samos, in the last century.
Because Ibykos[3] lives there. And I would track him down
To offer him a bottle of liqueur from the future,
So to drink with him and gaze at his incredibly strange face,
Which is remarkably like Brotachos'. And I would look at this face
And think, all at once, about the whole Constellation of Dioskouroi.[4]

And if I ever go to heaven, I wish there to be more
Hummingbirds there than there are here.
And I hope there is a tiny golden kind.
Because when this kind beats its impossible wings so fast,
The sound of Brotachos' voice comes out, making every poet
Want so much to be so good to every other one.

And if I could ever do something all over again in the City of Athens,
It would be to go to Brotachus' apartment in the Boat-making District.
Because it is like a boat, and Korax and Markos[5] and the one whose
Name on the list is number thirty are also there. And we will read
Poetry to the music of Demostratis, sure in the knowledge that
Storms and other dangerous weathers will not harm us.

And if I should ever give someone flowers again,
I hope to give them to Brotachos of Alkmena.
Because once when I brought him flowers, he put them
In a vase in the middle of his seven bronze muses,
And he closed his eyes and bent towards them, as if in prayer,
For a long time, and I saw two tears fall into the flowers.

Therefore, if I ever give him flowers again, I hope their
Aroma to be like a drug, unbounded by time.
Because we will sit together on his goatskin-covered
Couch, and look at a long scroll of Antimenidas' etchings.
And Brotachos will move his hand over all the parallel worlds curled
Up in there, making me want to fall asleep, and pick up exactly
Where I'd stopped in my dream, just as if I'd never left it.

And because I hope that when I wake, my head will be on
His shoulder, and his sleeping head will be resting
Lightly upon mine. And the scroll will still be open.

—Megaklys. The provenance and dates of the author of this extraordinary poem are unknown, though the reference to Ibykos "in the last century" would date it ca. fourth century. Intact papyrus discovered in Alexandria in the Montazah Palace find of 1998. No other works by him are known to exist.

[1.] Of course, the classical number is nine.

[2.] Nothing is known of this figure.

[3.] Great court poet of the tyrant Polykrates, from sixth/fifth century, B.C.

[4.] The constellation of good fortune for sailors, suggesting that Megaklys may have been a fisherman or mariner of some kind.

[5.] Neither of these two figures is known, nor are Demostratis or Antimenidas.

TIME

[Everything before this torn away, probably by a child, in great fury, for there is the silhouette of a mother, with the hint of something long and tubular in her mouth.]

would leave them,
ludicrously, like props on a stage:
Your crumbling tunic,
a silkworm's hollow cocoon,
the vanished cicada's husk,
Alkman's empty tomb:

Each woven, Megalostrata,[1]
in the patterned slough of time's skin,
that snaking and tubular thing. Gently
hold its shimmering tail and sleep:
Dream of a boy and a girl entwining
their lithe and sweating bodies.
And of the sky's dispassionate
face, the moon staring down,
like an eye whose lid has been shorn.

—Alkman, resident of Sparta, ca. seventh century B.C. While his extant work is almost wholly concerned with Spartan festivals and banquets, this poem, discovered at Montazah, demonstrates a metaphysical and tragic concern that has not been previously known.

[1.] Megalostrata was a woman poet and contemporary of Alkman, who seems to have been in love with her.

DEATH MASK

[Moths eating, their thorax's growing purplish and huge.]

lovely geography,
pushed out in this face,
but not upwelling from the earth below,
nor carved in relief from space above.
The form arrives from somewhere else

[Moths eating, their thorax's growing purplish and huge.]

—*Mimnermos, ca. seventh century B.C., resident of Smyrna or Kolophon. The above fragment most likely belongs to his elegies to Nanno, the flute-girl who accompanied the recitation of his lyrics. She was kidnapped and brutally murdered by Meniskos, a minor poet, who was intensely jealous of Mimnermos's fame.*

A GOD

Fear and joy,
love and rage,
sorrow and lust,
all of it molten
and pulsing from
within, forging
the body's chambered
form, like some incubated
god, writhing himself into being.

—*Timokreon, ca. fifth century B.C., visceral poetic rival of Simonides, was priest of a Dionysian cult and a great glutton. Simonides' epigram to him reads thus:*

After eating, drinking, and vomiting slander
to my heart's content, I lie here rotting,
Timokreon of Rhodes.

JOINTS

Joints are parts of the body and yet not parts of the body.
They join through opposition to create a harmony of autonomous
        forces.
Mountains arise because of the absence of mountains.
The absence of mountains arises because of the mountains.
Because neither exists without the other, neither exists in self-same
        identity.
This is also true of all flora and fauna, of all humans and all their deeds.
When we are awake we share a world.
When we are asleep, we are each in a discrete world.
This is, upon reflection, like the mountain and its absence.
This is also like words and their ideas.
Words are mountains; ideas are the absence around words.
Identity arises from discrete particulars; discrete particulars arise from
        identity.
Our understanding of the greatest matters will never be consummated.
All opposition is seamlessly interconnected by atomic joints.

—Herakleitos, fifth century B.C. Poem discovered in the Montazah Palace find. Herakleitos (Heraclitus of Ephesus) is, of course, one of the great philosophers of antiquity. His central proposition, that the fundamental condition of nature is change and impermanence, reflects, with remarkable synchrony, the first of the Four Noble Truths of Buddhism, as proclaimed by his exact contemporary, Siddhartha Gautama. In this poem, Herakleitos also seems to intuit the fundamental Buddhist truth of interdependence and non-identity.

A SINGLE MIND

1. A single mind is all things.

2. All things are a single mind.

[Large holes: Moths? American academics?]

10. Listen: One can never step twice in the same river.

11. Listen: In swallowing, the moon is brought forth.

12. Listen and spit out: The swollen moon is brought forth.

13. Swallow your self and swallow others.

14. Spit out your self and spit out others.

[Large strange holes, mysterious gaps, frightening loss.]

26. When clouds fly, the moon moves.

27. When a boat goes, the shore moves.

28. The boat and the shore travel at the same time, walk together, without floating or turning.

[Holes eaten by time, American academics, loss, and mystery.]

39. Listen: The reader and writer pass with their dragonfly bodies in the sky, while words, like clouds, float by.

40. Listen: the cloud's flying, the moon's traveling, the boat's going, the shore's moving, the reader's and writer's passing, these are not bound by past, present, or future.

41. Nor do they have any starting or stopping.

42. Not starting or stopping, not going forward or backward, the moon's movement is true and not true.

43. Because it is beyond beginning, middle, or end.

44. Therefore, one can never step twice in the same river.

45. Listen or not: A single mind is all things.

46. Listen or not: all things are a single mind.

—*Tantalos of Myrina, fifth century B.C. Discovered in the Montazah find. This is the only known writing by Tantalos of Myrina, who is mentioned by Herakleitos and other contemporaries.*

MISSION

We decamped from Pylos, barbarian town smack in a boulder field,
and set oar to lovely Asia, making fair Kolophon our base. We gathered
our strength for a fortnight, writing poems and sharpening our swords
by the sea. On the morning the oracle spoke in tongues, the main column
followed the rushing river through the forest, while our unit of ten went
      upward
and west, along a tributary stream. At a small waterfall we stopped to rest
on some moss, and gazed at our golden helmets and shields in the reflecting
      pool.
We spoke in low voices of the beauty around us, of the dark, darting trout
and of the strange, haunting songs in the towering trees. We spoke of time,
and friendship, and truth. Then each of us drank deeply from the pool.

Aided by the gods, we stormed Smyrna, and burned its profane temples
      to the ground.

—*Archilochos, seventh century B.C., soldier and one of Greece's greatest poets. He is credited with
the "invention" of iambic meter. Brief fragments of this poem have been translated previously.
The entire text was discovered intact in the Montazah find.*

REVENGE

[Blackened at top by time or fire, eaten yet above that by the lepidoptera, oh, my white village, like a mirage on the hill, when I remove the gauze from my eyes.]

that little hill, rubbed bald
by galling winds, the fossil-hill
nigh the Hades Hole.

We'll stitch chords to their ribs
and fly them like kites. We'll
chorus our dead to the music
of the humming strings.

[Gnawed away. Impossible to know if the poem ends here.]

—*Phillipos. Fragment discovered at Montazah. Nothing is known of this poet and apparent soldier. While we have titled the poem "Revenge," the identity of the 'body-kites' is not entirely clear: Are they enemies, as we have guessed, or fallen comrades? If the latter, the poem might be titled "Funeral," or "Afterlife."*

POETRY

[Rotted away.]

What [does] poetry do for the world?

[Rotted away.]

—*Anonymous fragment. Discovered in the Montazah find.*

APPENDIX: TWO LETTERS

10/ IX/ 02

Dear Mr. Johnson,

There is little time in this life for us to account for our sins. God is merciful in victory, but implacable in defeat. You must beg forgiveness without delay, commit the penance of the auto-Pharmakos[1] and the tongue-clamping measure of the Second Encyclical, thus surrendering yourself to Him with all the ounces of your will. Only in this way will you be cleansed of the murder of Alexandra (you know what I'm talking about) who was like a daughter to me, and like a sister to my brother monks.

What you have done is very grave. That you would ask me for a "blurb" to your "translation" compounds your serious sin.

Do you not know it yourself? And now you have stolen what little she had in her suffering life: You have stolen and lied your way into her mind and her poetry and thus into her and our true history. How dare you? Have you no shame? Is Poetry for you nothing but a game of evil to kill others? Meditate on this question until your head is attached to your corpse in a medical college (this is foretold by the Oracle).

Commit the additional repentances (seven times each day)[2] that I include in the enclosed brochure.

May our compassionate God have mercy upon you.

—Pan-Abbot Father Savvas

---

[1] According to Loeb (*Greek Iambic Poetry*, p. 359), "The *pharmakos* was an ancient form of purification as follows: If a disaster, such as famine or pestilence, or some other blight struck a city due to divine wrath, the ugliest man of all was led to sacrifice in order to purify and cure the city's ills. They set the victim in the appropriate place, put cheese, barley cake and dried figs in his hand, flogged him seven times on his penis with squills, wild fig branches, and other wild plants, and finally burned him on wood from wild trees and scattered his ashes into the sea and winds in order to purify the city of its ills." The "auto-Pharmakos" urged on me by Pan-Abbot Father Savvas would, I assume, be a modified version of the original.

[2] The number 7, for the seven holes of the human body, is of theological significance to the Greek Gnostic Order (Authentic Synod).

My Darling:

On March 14, I did find a conceptual praxis whereby morphemes, these so crazy particles that are the source of All Contradiction in the World of Signified Appearances (mat is mat because it is not bat; the Blogger man you spoke of, Kasey Silem Mohammad is Kasey Silem Mohammad because he is not William Carlos Williams), may be accelerated at opposite directions through connecting wormholes in the poem*, and at so much unbelievably fantastic speed, so that when they smash against the other, the names of Samothracean gods become released and scattered in paragrammatic traces, dashes, and spirals across [the] flattened phase-face of the poem . . . [Long pornographic tirade deleted here. KJ]

Hooded Authors wander through cork-screwed streets there, serenely greeting to other hooded Authors with a bow. The poets follow not what is outside the eyes, but what is within, "shimmering," as Althusser said in Lenin and Philosophy, "beneath the world." They are very dark from having gone out to the true edge . . .

Thus, all manner of Contradiction goes away. I am quite confident that the poets of Patmos, a thousand years hence, their hardened hair pulled back by Sacred Law to a sharpened point three feet behind their heads, will assume this as second nature.

Now, does this mean that Paradox is vanquished, also? No not at all, nor could it be. For Paradox is a higher manifestation of contradiction, and it clearly transcends contradiction. She is a gowned, beheaded Nike, [and] the feathers of her outspread wings curl round the furthest reaches of every figure of speech, thus gathering all difference back into the center of a Truth that is so near we are always overlooking it in our great anxiety to be "relaxedly classical," "universally personal," "casually cosmopolitan," or "opaquely experimental," whatever the case, yes? To see her ecstatic, headless form appear in holograph inside the poem puts a new spin on everything.

Alexandra

---

*Elsewhere, she writes: "These poetic wormholes are everywhere, actually, in any poem, regardless of the poem's contingent value or prosody, and at any phonemic point through whose tiny trumpet-like hole the whisper of lost, dead language puffs upward." KJ

Eight Imitations for *Trobar*

To John Bradley

— after Tu Fu's "To Pi Su Yao"

It's hard to know if we have talent. Here and there, a drunken
grad student expresses admiration. It's pathetic, really: our cars
are junk, missing half their hubcaps; in the place on our vitas
where the "prizes" should go—about the same number as the hubcaps.
The wheels start to fall off: beer bellied, flatulent, we've become
the objects, from afar, of our children's disdain. Twenty years beyond
the prime of life, inadequately covered, we buy Viagra with our overtime
pay. Who gives a fuck about either of us or our elected tribulations?
We've been reduced, here, at *Sullivan's Tavern*, to our own audience.
Though the workers from the tannery stare at us with contempt,
we appreciate each others' poetic merits. Our poems will be completely
forgotten, rot in the landfill of oblivion. With wry smiles and toasts
to the ancient ones, we console each other:

In that common, mass grave, we shall never be alone.

JULIAN IN NICOMEDEIA
—*after Cavafy*

Errant and ominous things, now.
As ever, exaltations for the rule of global free markets.

The supernatural visitations, the official State visits to ancient holy
sites of the heathens. A certain frisson for the gods of the mystic Orient.

The sub-rosa gatherings in the old days with Chrisanthius.
The daring war plans of Maximus—the torturer—a poet, besides.

But this is what it's come to: Gallus betrays chronic fidgetiness
and rashes. Constantius exhibits boils and symptoms of paranoia.

Ah, the advisors in the intelligence agencies don't look as sapient as
the media, the obscenely obsequious media, had made them out to be.

The situation—whispers Mardonius, the opposition's Speaker
in the Senate—is, like, really fucked up.

And even though we voted for War because we thought certain ancient
holy sites hid weapons of supernatural destruction,

some kind of disposition must now be made (with an expected measure
of hubris befitting imperium) to appease the heathens . . .

In the interregnum, oblivious Julian makes a campaign appearance at the
Colosseum of Nicomedeia, where at the top of his lungs and with a
            plebeian twang

he praises the charioteers and recites the Holy Scriptures, while the
            NASCAR
faithful acclaim, with roars, his Christian, his common-man authenticity.

An Unexpected Correspondence
—*after Jack Spicer*

Dear Mr. Johnson:

I have realized, suddenly, with a start, that I failed to include an important point in the first version of this, sent to you two years past. Now there is a bump on my head from sitting up so quickly and hitting it, hard. There is not much space between my bed and the ceiling, I'm afraid.

I believe I had said that through the gentle and waking-dreamed eyes of the good Kevin Killian, I have glimpsed the little blowtorch you have held against their Faces. Against the feces of my children. (note: "Feces," I see, is a typo in the first version, but no doubt you and the readers of the "Funny Business" issue of The East Village took it as a pun.) Anyway, as I said, All fucking by Poets takes place in Hell. And you will still need to learn how to write better. My enthusiasms.

I have also seen all of your invented letters. The ones from the living are quite boring. The more interesting ones are from the dead. (Even now, even after all the signs, Mr. Killian does not know I am looking through his eyes.)

There is not much time given for writing where I presently am. So I will tell you five things, and if you're smart, you will believe me and then pass them on:

1) The entire matter is a very complicated situation, more complicated than you can presently imagine.
2) You are right about their burned or smelly faces, but that will never mean you should not kiss the image of your own head.
3) Poetry is like a bump on your head, and the swelling will never go down, no matter how deep the kiss.
4) Poetry blogs are like oil wells, only with hair.
5) The scene now is New York, where there's a hundred foot statue of Frank O'Hara outside the MOMA, so you should move there.

Love,

Jack

33 RULES OF POETRY FOR POETS 23 AND UNDER

—after Nicanor Parra

1. Study grammar. Only by knowing grammar, knowing clearly the parts of speech and sensing their mysterious ways in sentence parts, will you be able to write interesting poetry. For poetry is all about grammar's interesting ways.

2. Don't suck up to other poets. Well, OK, you will do so, of course, like all poets do, but when you do, feel it in your bones. Take this self-knowledge and turn it into a weapon you wield without mercy.

3. Read the old Greeks and Romans in the original. Studying Greek or Latin is one of the best ways of becoming a man or woman of grammar. Well, Duh, as they say here in Freeport at Tony's Oyster Bar.

4. Ask yourself constantly: What is the fashion? Once you answer, consider that noun, participial, infinitive, or prepositional phrase (the answer will mutate over time) your mortal enemy.

5. Ask yourself constantly: What is the worth of poetry? When you answer, "It is nothing," you have climbed the first step. Prepare, without presumption, to take the next one.

6. Don't drink and drive. Better yet, just don't drink.

7. At the second step, should you reach it, don't look down: You might get dizzy from the height and fall into an alcoholic heap. Trust me.

8. Read Constantine Cavafy's great poem, "The First Step." Meditate upon it.

9. Don't worry if you have social anxiety at poetry events. Most everyone else will be as secretly anxious as you are.

10. Read Ed Dorn carefully, starting with *Abhorrences*, working your way back.

11. Remember that the greater part of it is merely show and acquired manners. Poets can be mean and they will try to kill you.

12. Ponder Bob Dylan's classic line: "I ain't gonna live on Maggie's farm no more."

13. After reading Roland Barthes's famous essay on it, watch professional wrestling at least once a month. Reflect on how the spectacle corresponds, profoundly, to the poetry field.

14. Go on your nerve, and whenever you feel you shouldn't, do.

15. Don't smoke cigarettes, even if you think it makes you look cool to others (or to yourself).

16. Go by the musical phrase and not the metronome. But when convenient, or just because it's beautiful, go by the metronome.

17. Don't let anyone tell you MFA programs are bad. MFA programs are really great—you can get a stipend and live poor and happy for two or three years.

18. Make sure you act like an insufferable ass in your MFA program. Never suck up to other poets. Traditional or avant-garde . . .

19. If you don't know another language, make it your mission, as I suggested earlier, to learn one. Translation is the very soil of poetry. Its mystery.

20. The Web is a wonderful development. Don't make yourself a slave to its "cool" corporation of the moment.

21. Whenever you are in doubt about being a poet, instead of, say, being an architect or a physicist, or something of the superior sort, remind yourself of Leibniz's immortal question: "Why is there something rather than nothing?" (Keep this question in your pocket against your heart. Because no one can ever answer it, it is the key to your purpose.)

22. Write political poems. But remember: The politics you are likely protesting are present, structurally, inside poetry, its texts and institutions. Write political poems with a vengeance.

23. Read Wittgenstein. Don't ever feign you understand him. He didn't understand himself! Steal from his genius ammo dump.

24. When someone tells you there are two kinds of poetry, one of them bad, one of them good, chuckle gently.

25. Don't ever use a Power Point® at a Conference on Innovative Poetry. Power Points make you look like a tool!

26. Remember what I said (sorry to be so pedantic!) about grammar. If you can't confidently analyze a sentence, forget about poetry. Poetry is the art of language, right? Well, if poets cannot be the experts on grammar, then something is wrong. A generalized disregard of linguistics and grammar, by the way, is one of the main reasons the so-called post-avant is in crisis. I'm dead serious.

27. If you feel you have wasted your young life so far writing poetry, that writing poetry was a fool's, a loser's pursuit, and you sense despair and absolute darkness before you, well, you are surely on the second step. There is no shame in turning back and leaving it all behind. Turn back without regret. On the other hand, if you are crazed and brave and you put your queer shoulder to the wheel, much wonder, blessedness, and inexpressible sorrow awaits.

28. Travel. Go to Asia, South America, Africa, Micronesia, North Dakota.

29. Read Eliot Weinberger, starting with both *What I Heard about Iraq* and *Karmic Traces*, working your way back.

30. Read Kenneth Rexroth's *One Hundred Poems from the Chinese* and *One Hundred More Poems from the Chinese*. If someone tells you there are two kinds of poetry, chuckle gently.

31. Look in the mirror and be honest. You are going to die. But right now you're alive . . . Look really hard. This is fucking astonishing. Why is there something rather than nothing?

32. Determine, as of now, that should you have children sometime, your devotion to poetry will somehow enrich their lives and not be a cause for their suffering. Listen to me and don't take this as melodramatic, middle-aged fluff. Quite a few kids have died for lack of what a poet found there.

33. On the third step, should you get there, its blank humming sound, realize this is almost surely the last step. Pump your legs up and down. Victory will be (as they used to say in the days of Deep Image

and Language, back when poetry was innocent yet) dark, opaque, and strange.

Prosodic Structure

—a bit after Barbara Guest

The first stanza exists so that the second stanza
may exist. There is no other reason to provide.

In this second one, now, we are climbing back up
through the hole of the reason inside the first. Where it
is darker than it first appeared. Where a soft sort of static
seems disseminated and everywhere. As if the mind
were an anther, its dehiscence whispering there, inside
a structure of no one's providing. We look around with
our ancient desire. We look to each other. We may exist,
we say. And we say so as we come, awkwardly, back down.

Thank you for putting your head up there with me.
Your guess, really, is as good as mine.

ENCOUNTER
—after Miłosz

Fleeting Presence now reading, pray imagine us there where you presently are . . .
      Tablet fragment, Sumer

We rode forever through great traffic in a sedan toward evening.
Blackhawks rose, blackly, against the sepia hue.

And promptly, the boy walked in all of his life across the street, holding
      against his chest a book purple or blue.
We looked at him holding the book with all of our sight.

This was thousands of years back. Thousands of years are nothing to
      the dead.
Not to the eveninged boy, nor to the ones, perfumed, who looked, longingly,
upon the world in its fleeting light . . .

O God who gave us strength, where are they, if ever they truly were,
      toward what,
truly, do they unfold or ignite:
The movements of the boy darkly crossing, the call to praise You rising,
      the righteous
verses ardently burning?

I ask You, yes, inside faith and sorrow, but more—my hand moving
      forever down, dopamined, to the detonator's head—
I mean I ask You, my Muslim, my Jewish, my Christian God, I ask
      in fear and infinite astonishment.

The Impropriety of the Hours
—after César Vallejo's 'La violencia de las horas'

The whole habitus has gone up in flames.

N. went up in flames: SHE, the bird-throated one, who cruised chat rooms and cooked jamush in the market on a kerosene lamp.

The mullah, G., combusted in a whoosh: HE, with the eyes of green tile, who loved the songs of boys in the madras, even as he scolded and shushed.

The red-haired one, K., became a fire fountain: SHE, with the plastic tree of buttons and business cards, who left behind a four-month old, who died without skin, floating in a plastic tub of melted ice, on the following day.

My sister-in-law, A., bizarrely flashed and vanished in brilliant light: SHE, of the yapping kennel of beings behind her mud house, and it was so sudden, like a search hit, while she bathed a brown dog who was bigger than she, sad dog of the mad doctor Dr. M., who'd renounced his Muslim name, and exploded in his bed, as he was weeping himself to sleep.

The young man with no legs and glass eye, whose name almost no one knew, though they called him S., became a hundred-foot flame: HE, who muttered the poems of Abu Nuwas, day after day, sitting in antique leather chair, with lawn-mower wheels, in front of tin shop of the watchmaker B., who also blew up, while tapping tiny gold hammer to tiny gold wheel.

J. burned slowly: HE, the blue-skinned dwarf, with a thing for Tom Cruise, for he gathered wild leeks on the outskirts of town, and when he was found he presented intact, so perfectly white, though the smoke that did drift from his eyes was the color of his skin, in his strange life.

My grieving brother, D., shot columns of fire-jelly out his bottom and mouth: HE, the clown on the side, in the peace of thighs, and the joy of small blogs, whom children would laugh at and mock, but who would fall silent, the children, at his fist-sized tears, making his the face they'd recall, when it faintly rained and the young thistles were in bloom.

My brother-in-law R., who was just visiting from An Najaf, became a sudden and inexplicably small puff of smoke: HE, of the Bedouin revolver and the cufflinks and the saws, which like my sister and her husband became confused with him by chance in a single dark thing, the three of them and the things, joined like a caravan spied from above, a digital smudge, in a valley of dull rocks, in a month of great heat, and in six unending years.

The hip-hop fan, M., dissolved like half a million into the great bonfire he became: HE, gigantic by the measure of our race, skull-faced, with stutter, who made people clap their ears, even as they gazed in stupor and awe, for it was he who called to prayer from the minaret, and it was said that such paradox was from God, was connected to the miraculous productivity of the hens of our town, who stopped their clucking at his call, and laid eggs that were translucent and huge.

Yes, the whole town has gone up in flames, and I am speaking of it now, inappropriately, in the on-line light, of this fun avant life.

Into the Heat-Forged Air

Far from the Rappahannock, the silent Danube moves along toward the sea.
—John Ashbery

Far from the Pirin, the pointy Appenines plummet toward the sea.
The grey and mauve Virungas undulate pleasantly, much like
The Darlings in their slumber. Chuckling nomads make lean-tos
Within the Schwatka. Troop carriers rust their wheels
On the Taurus, and jackals roam
The Toba Kakar. The Sentinel Range is white with
Dust, as are the peaks of the Ahaggar, covered in
Dust. The Tibetsi are grey and dry as bone.
The Sierra Madre is neither sentient nor unsentient.
Whilst the Titiwangsa appear to walk in the sky, the Verkhoyansk
Splash about in the sea. The Mackenzies are phlegmatic,
Almost diffident beneath their weathers.
Eons have crosshatched the Silvretta Alps,
Pure porphyry. Ophitic basalt predominates
In the Aberdare; its radiating crystals of feldspar recall
Dandelions in seed. Not so the Hafner Group, whose pure
Slate is uniform and dark. Slowly, the Koryak
Crash into the Kurai. The grave and dry Drakensbergs
Couldn't give a darn what anyone thinks, but
The Glarus crackle companionably in the sun. Bombers draw
Vapor circles over the Lesser Khingan. People die of thirst,
Fleeing over the unforgiving Rockies.
The Pegunungan have never been climbed,
Sheer and crumbly their needle peaks.
The Bergamo Alps are sheathed in mist. The Massif Central
Is imposing from afar, but palm-fringed are its valleys.
The Kunlun are huge. The Glockner Group tilts
Forward and laughs, like a girl at an angle, held up
By a gale, while the Rieserferner Group is one of
The shortest ranges of the world,
Likewise the tiny Angokel.
Still, the Sistema Penibetico goes on forever.

The Rhaetian Alps eat climbers like candy,
Yet the Cherangany are mild. In the Brooks Range, ferns
And cairns become abundant; giant sloths are joyous on the
Plessur. The Ratikon is all hollow, a carapace of slate.
The Wetterstein has a ruined tavern half-way up. If there is a
Geological example of neurosis it is the Brenta Group. Not so
Its neighbor, the Karawanken, serene and languorous in its smooth
Rock skin. Strangely, the Dolomites are made of limestone,
As are the Ortlers. Migrants trek down the Cottians, carrying
Torches. The Mont Blanc Group is famous; the Cairngorms are
Covered in primeval pine. The Caucasus are stern and dark.
The Carpathians span five countries, all once members of the
Warsaw Pact, but the Juna are smothered in crows and the roaring of
Caws. The Pyrenees are sullen, aloof, though this
Is all part of their insouciant charm. Even as the Altay turn to mud,
Night envelops the Nulatos. Chinamen jump with a thump
On the Jotunheimen, while the Sierra Morena blushes
In the evening, powdering its breasts with cloud. The Svecoffenides
Are lugubrious, a lure for poets. The Table Mountains are flat,
Awash in runic trash. No one can believe the Golden Mountains.
But the Stone Mountains are airy, made of chalk, tunneled and
Hollowed out like Swiss cheese. The Bystrzyckie Mountains are
Unknown, devoid of life, while the Urals are vast and crisscrossed
By capillaries of gold. The Vosges, avant-garde of ranges, has not
Much changed since the invention of photography. The Appalachians
Are growing smaller by the day. The Wicklow Mountains were once
A redoubt of the IRA; now they are mottled with ocotillo and
Mesquite. The Endless Mountains end abruptly on the outskirts
Of Harrisburg. Meth labs crumble like sandcastles in the Green
Mountains. Adult stores are buried under strata in the Smoky
Mountains. The White Mountains are full of wind. The East
Catches the light; the Rubies have knife-like ridges.
The Shoshone Range loves to whisper its name on the wind, and
True to its name, the Snake Range is full of them. The Toiyabe Range
Bakes its rocks under the superheated sun. The Endicott Mountains

Release their small snows, teasing the streams. More children are lost
In the Black Hills than any other range; at least half are found years
Later, in the shadows of the Punamints, mendicants with no
Memory of their pasts. The Anti-Lebanon is covered with checkpoints,
But not so the Otztals. The Tian Shan are so trodden, whole areas
Are like sponge; still, the Tatras are slick and hard. Deer bed down
In the Elburz with the lion. From above, the Hindu Kush look like
Sutures, raised and purple, along a thigh. Snowcranes turn to ice
On the Hida, blown upward by massive drafts; they fall like toys,
On the hot stones. Sunnis squat in caves in the Safed Koh; in every cave
A little cage, and in every cage a sparrow from the Alleghenies. Prayer
Wheels make clacking sounds in the Western Ghats. Strange concussions
Are heard deep inside the Zangezurs, though no one knows why.
The Vindhya Range is mute, intractable, along the spine of India:
How does consciousness arise? The Cordillera Darwin swarms
With thistles and ferns. Black helicopters fly over the Cordillera Negra,
Never to be seen again. The Cordillera de Lipez is hollow, its rock
Thin as eggshell. The Cordillera de Sarmiento is a block of stone.
The Sierra Ventana is covered in dust; it blinds those who would seek
Meaning in form. The Cordillera Pelada is covered in blue dust.
The Parcell Mountains are taut as a bass string, even when covered in dust.
UFOs hover over the Sandias. The Sierra Nevada is sprinkled with corpses,
Turned to quartz, while the Torngats have Sasquatch, otherwise known
As Bigfoot. The Superstitions are dotted with radio dishes, but tiny elk
Rut in the Kigluaiks. The Eje Transversal has nothing to say. The Anvil
Range smells like wild cabbage or fennel, and the Glenyon Range does
Too, though more subtly. The Bitterroot puckers its lips
In the rain, and the Cabinets hold many wonders. The Gallatin Range
Is lousy with moles; the Garnet, its sister, is 90% iron. The mountains
Are indifferent to our yearnings, our joys, and our sorrows.
The John Long Mountains look like a boy praying toward Mecca;
Bats prowl their starry skies. The Castle Mountains have
Been reduced to conglomerate clods of granite and chert,
A hilarious hulk of hubris. The Klamaths are retiring
And diffident, but no less noble for that. Great howling

Armies clash in the Ouachitas, but the Nadaleen Range
Is encased in dust. The Ozarks are conflicted between
Tradition and modernity, though the Chilkat Range
Is a lizard's dream. People climb the ten thousand paths
Of the Himalaya, seeking who knows what. On the Schober Group,
Lava flows upward and downward. The Niedere Tauern
Just sits there; no one knows its true nature. Amazingly,
The Lepontine Alps run upward and downward and in all directions.
After entering the Sumava, it is said not a single person meets another,
For there is only the activity of the Sumava.
Hands are pressed to cave walls deep inside the Anti-Atlas.
The Granatspitz are puny next to the Thurnwalds.
The Montes Rook, towering and hermetic,
Form the smiling mouth of the frozen Moon.

Seven Writings for *Locus Solus*

Am I the only idiot here, on this hill, surrounded, as I am, by rutting rams and heated ewes?

Our quaint and severe village is in the valley, there: the steeple and its blue bell, the round mud huts, washed white, their conical thatches, o. And the air? Why, the air is blue and clear as a bell.

A yodel comes up the hill, followed by another, in a slightly different pitch, though just as fair, for the practice there has worn them really about the same.

Why, it's my old pals from grad school, James Tate and Dean Young! They lie fornenst, on either side of me, face-up, hands locked behind their heads, under the puffy, cotton-ball clouds. I plunge my tongue to their bare-stript breasts.

Baa-a! says James.

B-aaa! says Dean.

Ba-aa! says I.

And then we laugh, and James rolls a bone the size of a cigar. We lean and loafe at our ease, playing the dozens with non-syllogistic sentences, so the paragraph becomes a unit of quantitye, not logick or argumente. Nay, we do not think whom we souse with spray.

By and by, a third yodel rolls up the hill, this one deeper and more complex than any yodel we have heard before, its fractal ironies unmistakable to our finer ears.

Why, it's our teacher from grad school, John Ashbery! He ambles towards us, with his slightly quizzical, diffident gaze, holding the tiny hand of his boyfriend, the Nut-Brown Maid.

Hey, did you guys see the fire? he asks, matter-of-factly.

No, sire, we say, What fire?

Look, he says, pointing, like Lenin, down to our tiny town.

From the mud huts, washed, as I'd said, in their white, puffs of smoke rise from the little flues. But there from a dwelling that is pretty much like the others, yet a little more towards the edge of town, flames shoot from the roof, thousands of feet into the sky.

O, it's the house of the Hejinians! we cry.

Aye, the East catches the light, and the history of poetry repeats its basic dialectic, endlessly, says John, cryptically.

We squint and espy the ant-like people, running around or passing water buckets in a line. And there goes the little red fire truck, speeding towards its fire, pulled by Gertrude, the ancient Clydesdale.

The Nut-Brown Maid yawns, pulls out his birding binoculars and hands them to me:

Aha! Russell Edson sits there, hunched like a gnome, gripping the reins, screaming something like Go horse Go!

In his pocket is his heart. It is *The Best American Poetry*.

SESTINA: AVANTFORTE

O your perfect, vulgate, hairy sestina
  —David Shapiro (correspondence with the author)

It's interesting how no one has yet written a sestina about John Ashbery,
Joseph Ceravolo, Barbara Guest, James Schuyler, Frank O'Hara, and
        Kenneth Koch.
After all, the New York poets wrote a bunch of sestinas, and Frank O'Hara,
of course, though he never wrote one himself, dropped the names of
        poets in his poems like crazy. James Schuyler
did too. He lived at the Chelsea amongst wackos of all kinds. Once, on
        the morning of this poem, when seven thousand saffron panels
        billowed in the park, on a day you could take up the tattered
        shadows off the grass, Barbara Guest
knocked on his door with a flat shape under her arm. Joseph Ceravolo

answered the door. What are you doing here, she said. Maybe I should be
        asking you that question, said Joseph Ceravolo.
Well, I've got this painting, it's by Joe Brainard, I wanted to show it to
        Jimmy, and it's called "Tangerines." John Ashbery
gave it to me after Frank O'Hara died, said Barbara Guest.
What do you mean Frank died, cried Joseph, I just saw Kenneth Koch
down at the San Remo, and he didn't say anything about that! Ha ha hee
        hee, laughed James Schuyler,
arranging some jonquils in the kitchenette, you two are a stitch and a half!
And they all laughed and laughed, like a happy rain, because the world was
new, and irony was so straightforward then, in the Kennedy era. And just
        then the phone rang. (It was Frank O'Hara!)

You'll never guess what, Jimmy, said Frank. What, Mr. Frank O'Hara?
said Jimmy, with a mock ceremoniousness. Well, don't tell Joe Ceravolo
because I want to tell him myself, and don't tell Kenneth, either, because
        you know how he takes these things, but they are here from
        Holland to make a movie about me. Can you believe it? Oh my
        God, Frank, squealed James Schuyler,
I *can't* believe it, that is so fantastic, and even though I am a bit envious, I
        am happy, too, but please can't I tell John Ashbery,

he'll be thrilled, he loves everything Dutch, in fact he just won some
        prize, and he might go there, and I'll tell him not to say a word
        to Kenneth Koch . . .
Joseph and Barbara exchanged quizzical looks. Jimmy, what the hell are
        you talking about, demanded Barbara Guest,

who was still standing there in the doorway holding her painting like
        some acoustic panel waiting for sound. Oh, Barbara, do be a
        good Guest
and come on in, said Jimmy, in his famous punning way, It's Frank O'Hara,
and they're making a movie about him, and it's all in Dutch, O poor
        Kenneth Koch,
he'll go mad like King George the Third, he's always wanted to be
        translated into Dutch! Actually, interjected Joseph Ceravolo,
he's just been translated into Swedish, by a countess from Minneapolis.
        A man shouldn't complain . . . The sun went behind a small cloud.
        Barbara was absentmindedly running her fingers across the
        inscription W.H. Auden had written for Jimmy in a first edition
        of *Some Trees*, by John Ashbery,
it said: To my friend in Foetry and all other things, Mr. James Schuyler.

(signed) W.H. Auden. The sun came out again and gently burned the
        world. James Schuyler,
she said coyly, in a Katherine Hepburn kind of way, do you think he said
        Foetry on purpose, or is that just his handwriting? Barbara Guest,
said Jimmy, clearing his throat and replying in formal kind, I've tried to
        figure that one out myself, it seems almost like a pun, doesn't it,
        and when I asked John Ashbery
himself, he got all distant and mysterious as a girl in a Vermeer, so I just
        don't know. By this time, Frank O'Hara
was beginning to wonder what had happened to Jimmy, who had become
        so distracted by the conversation with Barbara he had simply
        forgotten about Frank, and because he was on his lunch hour and
        had to meet Leroi Jones at the Automat, Frank decided to hang
        up. Joseph Ceravolo

said, Um, Jimmy, you kind of left Frank hanging, didn't you? Just then, Kenneth Koch,

still in his twenties (or so he claimed), came bounding up the stairs, crying out the names of northern European cities, the energy in and around him so electric, it looked like he could take it off and put it back on, like clothes. It's Kenneth Koch! said Joseph. Hi Kenneth! said Barbara, it's so nice to see you! Hello? Hello? Frank? Frank? said James Schuyler.

From my window I dropped a nickel by mistake, said Kenneth, looking fixedly at the floor and nearly shouting, **so I raced down and found there on the street, instead, a good friend, who says to me, in Dutch, Kenneth, do you have a minute? And I say, Yes! I am in my twenties! I have plenty of time! And so he tells me he's been translating my poetry, and it's going to be published! In Holland!** Jimmy quickly hung up the receiver and a look of absolute panic came down over his face. Joseph Ceravolo

(for this was a gift he had as a person and as a poet) radically changed the subject with the swift and elegant authority of a guillotine: Well, Kenneth, that is so fantastic, and even though we are a bit envious, we are happy, too. But look at this wonderful painting Barbara Guest

has brought to show us . . . Kenneth looked up. **You have TANGERINES in it**, said Kenneth. **And hey, by the way**, he literally yelled, as he started to do jumping jacks at a great velocity, **What's up with Frank O'Hara?**

Wait until he hears about Holland! Last time I saw him he said he felt like he'd never write again! I'm writing a lot, though! So where's he been? Huh? Uh, said Jimmy, he's, uh, been editing a new, um, sestina . . . full of, you know, cartoon characters . . . by John Ashbery . . .

Kenneth Koch's eyes got big as pool balls. **A *sestina*? A sestina by the poet of "The Tennis Court Oath," John Ashbery?**

Yes, said James Schuyler, nervously lighting a Gaulois, uh, W.H. Auden
   suggested he try one . . . I think . . . Just then, the phone rang
   again. Joseph Ceravolo, who was nearest the death-black
   machine, answered. Hi Joseph, the pleasant voice said. Was that
   Kenneth I heard shouting right before I hung up? (It was Frank
   O'Hara!)
Ah, hi, uh, no, no, there is no, ah, Olivia Oyl who lives here. Sorry.
   Goodbye. Click. The backs of all the chairs were turned towards
   the sun, and then Kenneth, past his seventieth jumping jack,
   started to get this feeling of exaltation. **And! But!** he yelled.
   He yelled so loud, it was as if the conjunctions could couple,
   like in the form of a centaur, the living to the dead. Now wait
   a second, they asked for *Olivia Oyl*? I mean, you've got to be
   fucking kidding me, said Barbara Guest.

.

DEAR EAGLES (2)

This earth will grow cold one day,
not like a block of ice
or a dead cloud even
but like an empty walnut it will roll along
    in pitch-black space . . .
You must grieve for this right now . . .
            —from "On Living," by Nazim Hikmet

your country's over. And though you're still here,
you will surely go.

For I have seen few snowmen outlast the snows.
            —from "Dear Eagles," by Gabriel Gudding,
                The Canary

I want to say that I have been reading the poem addressed to you,
the one soaring above all the others in the yellow canaried wood.
(You know how to trim your feathers to the fickle wind, O eagles!)
Before I had read the poem about you, I was whistling a tune about
snow, and holding a steak over my swollen eye (never read Lorca in
El Falangista Bar), thinking that my own poem was the bestest
in the whole diorama, a falcon to the little caged birds, opening their
little beaks to sing their beautiful, wind-up songs for their keepers.

Jeepers, I saw the title, "Dear Eagles," and first I thought it said
"Dear Faggots" (hard to read with one eye!), and I laughed like a cop
jilted by his blonde, took a swig of my breakfast beer, and behind my
steak saw the image of a saint all tied up, pierced by seventeen arrows,
his compassionate bovine eyes rolled ecstatically toward the sky. O,
maybe he was imagining me reading the poem about soaring You, as I
held a piece of Him against my battered, hallucinating eye. And then I
            read.
And then I read again.

And then I put down the flesh, and opened my third breakfast beer, and I
cried, cried heavily like Nazim Hikmet (grieving communist bard!), at
            the beauty

and the sadness of eagles, gone anon for always from the blackened
    walnut of
the world, world circling a collapsing sun, with no daughters or sons,
    or alcohol,
or any blue cars that drive, with poet faggots like me, and Nazim, and
    Gabriel,
through the stars. Nothing. Nothing there at all. I love you, eagles,
    though you will
surely go. And as I go down to my urn-shaped boat, to go speeding all
    lonesome
away, softly beat, please, your weird, snowman wings, over my silly pain.

EPISTLE TO DAVID SHAPIRO

[undated]

Dear David [Shapiro],

Yes, it's true, the Language poets air-brushed me out of Leningrad. One thing I will never forget from that simulacral city in reverse is sitting in a vast hall in a vast, ornate czarist building made all of marble, crimson-draped windows towering to the ceiling, looking out onto the Neva, swarms of cherubs fat and hot for Aphrodite above, a U.S. avantist facing me across the great mahogany table in a kind of late pinkish glow, dapper Aeneas in a polo shirt, looking somewhat edgy, eating little spoonfuls of caviar, as satyr attendants from the Ministry of Culture rose and offered formal toasts to the "American Poetic Friends of the Soviet Union."

Arkadii Dragomoshchenko leaned over to me and with booze on his breath said in heaviest accent, "Is this a great quantity of such repulsive fucking dog shit or what?"

"You think so?" I burbled, my mouth full of bread and sturgeon eggs. "Why, it's the first time in my life that I feel like a real Poet . . . I think this is fantastic!"

And to my left, far away, at the far head of the regal table, was another Language poet, his whole face consumed by a blinding sphere of light.

I ONCE MET DMITRI PRIGOV

I once met the great Russian Conceptual poet Dmitri Prigov. This was in Leningrad. The weather was warm, breezy, spectacular. We stood outside the old, elegant Hall of Composers. The street was torn up, and the great, jagged chunks of concrete made it seem the S.S. Leonid Brezhnev icebreaker had come through. I also imagined it looked like Stalingrad, during the siege. I have a gift for you, said Dmitri Prigov, and he handed me a manila envelope. O, thank you, Dmitri, I said, what is it? I opened the envelope and peered inside. Barrett Watten, solemn of visage, leaned his head over my shoulder, trying to squint inside, too. I pulled out seven, no, nine small stapled bundles, each with a typed word or three on the outside. What is this, Dmitri, I said. Ah, he said, They are Little Coffins of Poems, and inside each is a poem, but these little coffins may never be opened, for this would be of course disrespectful to the deceased . . . His friend Ilya Kabakov regarded me diffidently, dragging on a cigarette, looking something like a cross between a Czarist nobleman and a shipyard welder from Vladivostok. Perhaps he daydreamed, there, of his great future work, the installation of the shattered bedroom, the ceiling blown outward, a massive rubber slingshot suspended from it, like a giant jockstrap, the work he would entitle, The Man Who Launched Himself into Space . . . Then I went inside, with Michael Davidson, a very nice man, a true gentleman, and we peered at crinkly, yellowed scores under glass, drafts of music in Tchaikovsky's hand.

I ONCE MET STEPHEN RODEFER

I once met Stephen Rodefer. This was in England. It was Spring, and I was talking pleasantly to Kevin Nolan, Astrid Lampe, and David Bromige. Stephen Rodefer came over and said something like, So Kevin and David, is Eager Kent trying to suck up to you so he can make it in the avant-garde biz? He walked away, smirking, drink in hand, and I followed him down to the wine box. I grabbed his collar, pinned him against the wall, and said I would break his impertinent nose and worse if he ever messed with me that way again. I mean, I was really angry! OK, OK, he said, I won't, take it easy man, take it easy . . . Later that day, he read a long diatribe against Language poetry and the post-avant. Midway through his reading, a nine or ten year old boy, a beautiful boy, truly, son of a Spanish poet there, it turned out, walked into the room. And I am not making this up: The boy sat down in a chair against the wall of the side aisle, about twenty feet from the stage, looked at Rodefer and smiled at him in the fullest, the purest sense one could ever give to a smile. I at first thought this must be Rodefer's son, for I saw that he stopped and beamed a huge smile back at the boy, and when he went back to read after a few seconds of just smiling at him, while the boy smiled back in turn, when he went back to read, that is, his poem about the complicities and hypocrisies and treacheries of the post-avant, he choked up and began to weep. He wept as he read, catching his breath in great gulps, sobbing his way through the savage invective of his piece (an invective now swathed in the soft raiment of a most powerful sorrow). And I noticed that the boy, poor thing, was totally confused and upset by this, he didn't understand (and neither did anyone!) and so he ran, embarrassed, out of the room. After a spell, Rodefer took a deep breath, straightened his back, wiped his eyes, and continued, energetically, as if nothing had happened. It was later that night I learned that his own son, aged ten, had drowned, in Paris, three years back. And the person who told me this said that Rodefer's son looked uncannily like this beautiful boy from Spain. And so I cried that night, back at my modernized room at Christ's College, a room, it was, down the hall from Christopher Marlowe's old purported room, and I cried for a long time. And the next day I went over to Stephen, by the wine box, and put my hand on his shoulder, and said, That was one fine, powerful reading you gave yesterday. And he turned and said Thanks, that's very kind of you to say. And we made awkward small talk for a while, and we walked out into the courtyard together, where it was cool in the evening air.

ORIENTALIST HAIBUN (with Cups of Sake Four)
    —for Alan Sondheim

It is because what we say is unfinished, always, that we can say
without fear. The gatekeepers themselves, in speaking back law, say
only what they have been given to say by signs. It is always
unfinished. Thinking of this I gathered courage, making prostrations.
The land to the East or West of us is there because we are here,
speaking of it. (Bill Berkson wrote that.)

Anyway, when I arrived at the first gate, I was told I could not
pass. The guards were dressed in coats of black scales, with
half-moons of gold covering their mouths. They spoke in tongues from
the West and told me to return there. Beyond their head-sets, sparks
flew in the night across the wooden houses, and I imagined that those
of the foreign community inside were shimmering and transparent
so that their bones mingled as one with the tea-fires and the frozen
flight of the cranes. (Awkward, but I am writing quickly here.) And
then, by magic, Mack, the Western Guards became tethered to long and
shiny poles of discourse (though it was dark and I couldn't quite
see) and were spun round and round so that a breeze lightly scented
with bream and salt cooled my face. I smashed the turtle's shell and
passed boldly through the gate.

You see, it was the thought of Witter Bynner that led me on. I
desired my dust to be mingled with his, forever and forever and
forever. I also thought of the following things, though I would never
dare to speak them openly:

The State of Hand Not Joined to Body
The State of Being Perfectly Not Here
The State of Disconsolate Thought of Wings
The State of Myouka Writing "Hand Not Joined to Body"
The State of Rose of the Snow Kimono
The State of Poem Written on Throat of Turtle
The State of Shikantaza as Loving Cunt Enfolding
The State of Kissing Son on Loving Lips

The State of Sons as Suicidal Aviators Exultant
The State of Being a Staff or Whisk
The State of Stillness in Self-Fulfilling Samadhi
The State Where the Moon Swallowing Is Brought Forth

Weary, I took a piss, making great steam in the Autumn grasses. Then,
preparing ink on a large stone, I wrote:

[xx] *shungyo ya hito koso shirane kigi-no ame* [xx]
Which I choose to translate thus:
[mourning his son he crosses the hills with a large sack of eggs]

When I arrived at the second gate, Chuck, it was May, and all was in the
State of Three Heads and Eight Arms as Rain on the Trees. The guard
of this gate had the corpulent face and body of Amida, but I knew
that was just a disguise. He spoke in hoarse whispers and in a
language I could only understand by imagining. He told me to display
wares in my lacquer-bone-poet-box, and I did so. He told me to
ornately describe the Eastern Suburbs with their alleys full of
squatting whores and peddlers, and I did this. He told me to squat
thusly and shit in my beggar's hat and I did so. He told me to write
one wonder-haiku on cicada husk's soundless cry, and I did this, his
sword suspended in threat above. I wrote:

Towa x ni x ikitashi x onna-no x koe x to x semi-no x ne x to
Which I choose to translate thus:
[my soul passes through those of others: hydragena exhibit]

Thus, this apparition vanished, and I went deeper into the mandala,
having no idea where I was headed (and admittedly half-wishing I had
heeded the cautionary advice of my grad school advisors). Wide-eyed,
I witnessed:

The Room of Looking through a Bamboo Tube
The Room of Scholars Who Count Letters

The Room of Poets with Strings of Law Leading Back to Their Names
The Room of the Theory of Five Ranks
The Room of Mud Within Mud
The Room of Merely Being "In the Mountains"
The Room of Oneness Within Differentiation
The Room of Udumbara in Shameless Flower
The Room of "Life Streams Issue from Plum Blossoms"
The Room of Everyday Rice-Eating Activity
The Room of Sky with Palms Together
The Room of Mind Moon Alone and Full

I felt fear and trembling, I felt the insistent repetition of all
phenomenal things, I felt an anxiety and dread of concepts that
verged (is it possible to say it?) on the irony of Being itself, and
I felt a sickness unto death. You see, Dick, I had come to
the gate through which the masts of Foreign Ships are visible! It was
like a forest after a great fire, or a city of people who have been
burned to a crust but are still standing. And I realized that this
was the Room of No Turning Back.

The guard here was dressed in elegant suit. He both was and was not
(if you can imagine that!) like the brittle sumi-e I had seen at
Eihei-ji: a single Not-Thinking stroke bringing sudden form out of
no-form. He appeared to me as an American executive from Toshiba, and
he brandished a scroll of unfair treaties, all inscribed in the most
delicate calligraphy. He said I could pass only should I beat him in
Poetry-Duel-to-Death. "I go first," he growled, "and my poem is
titled 'State of Siege.'" He read in rapid-fire bursts, his voice
screeching as ten-thousand shikirichi, and through the great roar of
rushing waters' sound, this is what I heard:

shaving dace [...] now stomping [.........]
town wall [....] place for gossip or [...]
[.......]daughter's dream–silkworm dealers?[.......]but[..]
But [......]market flooded. Why Pentium Chips if

[............]waving fan–clay stove [..]
[...............] so [....................] no, [................]
Ah, Hiroshima's blessing [...] fast track is [.......] better and
[.] for one thousand vats of nightsoil [................] but legs
spread for love-making [.........] while far away [.......]
geisha expert [...] quick web-search for [..........]
thirty seven Mexicans suffocated in freight car clawing eyes out
[...]

I was fearful and trembled at his fierce visage. A device for
measuring time glowed with Oriental splendour on his wrist. Sparks
flew in the night across the great wooden ships beyond. I knew now
the foreigners had been waiting there, Jack, shimmering and transparent,
for thousands and thousands of Springs. I dipped my brush and raised
it slowly back, knowing death-poem in my bones, knowing the darkness
there in the glistening point of it . . . And I wrote:

xHyakuxxxsen-noxxxdokanxxitsumademoxxxxwarauxxxkareno-nox
Which is untranslatable thus:
[   ]

————————

And when I woke, drenched from the dream, it was my teacher, serene
in Electric State of Coming Wonders, speaking to us in measured and
instructional tones. And this is what I heard:

"This paradox cannot be mediated, for it depends specifically on
this: In attachment blossoms fall, and in aversion weeds spread. The
single individual is only the single individual. As [inaudible] as
this single individual wants to express his absolute duty in the
universal, becomes conscious of it in the universal, he recognizes
that he is involved in a spiritual trial. [extended inaudible
section] Do not be limited to the narrow views held by human beings.
Even where there is no sun and moon, there is day and night."
(I taped that.)

He was a monk from Japan. He was vegetarian and ate his rice and things with chopsticks, Kent. And I spoke every Orientalist dream that came to me that sesshin, into the black hole of his succulent, papery ear.

Seven Submissions to the War for *The World*

BAGHDAD

Oh, little crown of iron forged to likeness of imam's face,
what are you doing in this circle of flaming inspectors and bakers?

And little burnt dinner all set to be eaten
(and crispy girl all dressed with scarf for school),
what are you doing near this shovel for dung-digging,
hissing like ice-cubes in ruins of little museum?

And little shell of bank on which flakes of assets fall,
can't I still withdraw my bonds for baby?

Good night moon.
Good night socks and good night cuckoo clocks.

Good night little bedpans and a trough where once there was an inn
(urn of dashed pride),
what are you doing beside little wheelbarrow
beside some fried chickens?

And you, ridiculous wheels spinning on mailman's truck,
truck with ashes of letter from crispy girl all dressed with scarf for school,
why do you seem like American experimental poets going nowhere
on little exercise bikes?

Good night barbells and ballet dancer's shoes
under plastered ceilings of Saddam Music Hall.

Good night bladder of Helen Vendler and a jar from Tennessee.
(though what are these doing here in Baghdad?)

Good night blackened ibis and some keys.
Good night, good night.

(And little mosque popped open like a can, which same as factory of
flypaper has blown outward, covering the shape of man with it (with

mosque): He stumbles up Martyr's Promenade. What does it matter
who is speaking, he murmurs and mutters, head a little bit on fire.
Good night to you too.

Good night moon.
Good night poor people who shall inherit the moon.

Good night first editions of *Das Kapital, Novum Organum,*
The Symbolic Affinities between Poetry Blogs and Oil Wells,
and the *Koran.*

Good night nobody.

Good night Mr. Kent, good night, for now you must
soon wake up and rub your eyes and know that you are dead.

WHEN I FIRST READ ANGE MLINKO

When I first read Ange Mlinko in *The Poker*, I started to bat
my eyes, seductively. Wow, I drank, this makes me want
to both write more and drink less so I might live longer! She's
fantastic!
My beautiful wife (for she is beautiful to me) yelled up the
stairs: "It's time for your date with the grill, Buster Lazy
Brown!" That was funny, my yelling wife, precisely
as a whole flock of Rose-breasted Grosbeaks settled
like a doubled harpsichord in the tulip flowering
by the jacarandas in the dying light. I'm not making that
amazing scene up, even though to you it may seem like I am, from "here."
But no, for I will say
to
you:
It was truly extraordinary, what I saw and heard inside that sudden gift—
luxuriant
spring efflorescing into a drug-like aureole, as if
it
    were
          some
              message
                    from
                         beyond,

which I know
it wasn't. And I know it doesn't fit in this poem, and that forcing it in will
likely hurt its chances for print, (not to mention these completely irregular
and
illogical
line-breaks!), but
for no reason at all, totally unbidden, in all that flocked music and gilded
light, I remembered
reading, as a passing mention in a buried article somewhere, of four little
girls incinerated in a mud compound by a missile fired from a pilotless
drone,

a compound in a dry and lonely place, where fine carpets were made by
orphans
for the foreign trade. I know
it's possible I'm just writing that I thought this then so to suggest my moral
sensibilities to you, using a tragedy that is not mine to give some moral
pressure to a poem
that
     up
         until
              now
                    hadn't
                         been

about much at all. I admit
I am not sure myself! And I admit that my having
written it means nothing, anyway, in the end. But the girls did
die, "were evaporated," at least that's what the little article said, and no
matter how self-
reflexive I get, or
how suspicious you become of my quaint
and insecure prosody,
those dirty-haired,
often-raped
       kids
          will
              still
                  be
                      dead

and never thought about again, by you or anyone. O,
the Grosbeaks sang for a spell and then
the Grosbeaks flew in a rush away, and I sighed, theatrically, like a bad
actress, a bit on purpose. I
don't know why I did so, just one of those campy outburst things you'd
never do

in public, I suppose, lest you lose a portion of your cultural capital, irremediably.

Anyway, there you have it. That's "my story." I slapped *The Poker* shut, waddled downstairs, and
threw
a match
on the fuel-soaked
briquets.

GREEN ZONE RENSHI-RENGA

—by Jack Kimball and *Kent Johnson*

There's no description I can give but the lion took the eagle's wings yet kept his own name.

If he could speak, would we understand him, you looking out in the rain from this image, ruins stretching for miles beyond the frame?

It is dark here, the houses a muted splash of vin blanc, the wind rolling down out of the thunder of jets.

What is the source of all this foil, this blue and gold tile, glimmering amidst the bodies of the penitent?

The lower floors coming down the garden steps in heels, a steel building and golden boa blowing kisses to the trees.

In the Courtyard of Ghazals, he whispers to the night-goggled guard, "How you know in religious city of strict forms when sexy boys do cross-dress, huh? Ha! You see, lovely American nervous boy? Ha!"

Follow the spiders, then let's dig ourselves out of the careworn, radiant footage—picture how melon in a box feels, the glow pruned, our molecules vibrating.

Let the call to prayer rise over this wet, crumbling city, and then let them walk secretly toward each other as martyrs do.

Clay funnels, whirlpools o' rain, such obstinacy! mirrored by the appetite of the almond-eyed filling the maverick mullah with sighs.

Back at the barracks, he writes longingly to him: "There's nothing I'd like more than to be the fuck out of this hell-hole, just be together at a bar, half-pound cheeseburgers with curly fries and a bucket apiece of ice-cold beers."

Tuscany or carbs? The other reclines, fearing his own share of attention is torn or, more, stapled to the city and its reinforcements that stand erect tonight, only dimly revealed.

Still, under the veil of a burkha, boys from Nebraska are naturally ambiguous through night-vision goggles worn by the other.

During the Staci regime Marsden and the others garnered precious little praise from their hard-line contemporaries. Perhaps this is why Sergeant Benezra disappeared during the A Minor Sextet.

Could you tell me, Raed, where I might find the Alley of Names, the one leading to the gauze-walled room at the heart of the bazaar, where orientalists like me are alchemized into melodious golden birds the size of an infant's thumb?

Your call is important to us but there's been a twist on the razing of the city: Benezra has overdosed, thus the demise of the most terrifyingly diminutive patron of witchcraft and psilocybin. Raed coughs up no response, blurring as the Alley does the boundaries between silk mosaic and Utopian gauze.

This collateral boy, the handmade kite intact, his limbs snapped off like straw, the stunned father gathering them up, calling his name . . . oh Poet, listen to this question in a muqtadab followed by a mujtathth: Would you forsake your poetry, all of it, all its pleasures and terrors, to make him whole again?

Before you answer, though, go approximately a mile, pass five mail slots on the boy's left, collect the terra cotta and other rewards that mount at your garden portal; your song is sung; go now, Poet, claim his stringbean body, and remember, make it look like an accident.

He woke from the dream of slitting the gauze and the ten thousand birds flying free to swarm like loving bees all over the boy's scrubbed and sutured form.

"Oh, yeah, baby, I'll listen to you—" a 'canonicity' of practical concern washed over the cornhusker's feral expression but then ("Oh, yeah") he forfeited all caution lifting the younger orphic frame, aglow even if lifeless, "I'll listen to you all night long."

The one with the robes spoke through a stuttering translator, whose words were then rephrased by a ban-rayed linguist from Special Forces, whose rephrasing was approved, in turn, with an indecisive nod by the stuttering translator: "Farm boy," said the one with ban rays, rephrasing what the other with the robes had haltingly said, "think of it this way: You have a shovel next to an upside down urinal in a museum; we have a giant black box in a desert with a black meteor at its core." The translator took this in, made an unpleasant guttural sound, and then his eyes rolled back all white into his head.

Puzzling and at times goofy expressions emerge from the countless layers of tapestry, squeezing starlight into an open-ended abstraction of laughter, at first, and then tears and quilt-like gloom. Marsden had come to terms with Raed, but hardly vice versa. On closer inspection the mullah honcho began to favor the Aussie over the farm hand. "Fuck him," Marsden quipped, filling the proceedings with a pointillism of gooey, sensuous intellect.

"But in truth we are always on the same page, as it were, even when we are in different worlds," said the almond-eyed one who had not yet spoken. He reached into the large terra cotta urn, delicately retrieved a common-looking cylinder seal, and held it up, turning it slowly against the light of the museum's seven mile high flames, revealing (to Marsden's utter, vertigo-inducing astonishment) the lost Sumerian map of the infinite poetic dimensions. "OK," said the latter in a meekish voice, "I take that back . . ."

Keepers of the Courtyard would have none of this, but their aplomb suddenly unwinds as Raed, blessed Raed, now awakes, bursting with song to that slender, younger form in the wings, "I suffer from insomnia, from loneliness I sleep, 8 TVs broadcasting in the midst of talk and laughter, wordplay and video all at once you are here—"

"Don't lose sleep over the 'noise,' my sweet qasida al-nathr," she said through the cell phone to the addressee. "Even in all the major world religions, the relation of syntax and linear thought to the holy is a matter of considerable dispute." And then she pushed *End* and evaporated, along the axis, into the infinite dimensions.

Her moniker came back to him as in an inspiration to dance, her moniker is Marsden, Marsden is she, four, five, glide, bow, whoosh. He, himself nameless, but lustrous, knew now deep inside, shaken to the core of his Nebraskan belief system, he felt the origin of space is named girls.

"Speaking of Courtyards named 'The Gestures of the Girls,'" said the pubescent Marsden with brother's brains on her first bra to him, "have you seen the Erratum card for "Fantasia on 'The Nut-Brown Maid'"? I know it by heart: 'Due to an unfortunate typesetting error, a line has been printed in an incorrect position. Line 6 on page 83, "falling back to the vase again like a fountain. Responsible" should be deleted. It appears in the correct place on page 88.'" Then the girl put her flowering forehead against the transparent tree and closed her almond eyes, seemingly oblivious to the gunfire and screams. "The big question we might want to consider," she continued, "mediated as we are by all these elaborately embedded 'quotations' is, 'Does it make a difference'?"

"Who gave woman this mouth?" The lion wears his wings on his head as a symbol of dubbined freedom. He walks the grassy ridge waiting for an updraft to lift him roaring into the sky. His growl is murderous. It translates into more language: "Judge not before I slit your eyes looking for a muse, gazing into who my mother was, a pathetic darkness splintering all of light." The lion looks to where the oaks once swayed, "I'll come no closer, for this space between woman and man is holy ground, a heather brush for killing in the stillness of bloodied heads and torn limbs."

Figures of the carousel lay scattered like junk on the grounds: The lion with broken wings, the lamb with the face of a boy, the horse with fire coming from his nose, the camel with his entrails of gold, the bird with the half-body of a girl, the see-through bull with the soul of honey, the torturer with the eyes of blue tile, the forged poet with the turban of stars, the fish with the scales of children's skin, the giant hermaphrodite with his sword of sky and her purse of streams. It used to be they all went around and around, to music and joy and quaint mechanical sounds. Now they are just banal figures of a carousel, scattered like junk on the grounds.

Then the breezy, lukewarm rockabilly starts up, and everyone yawns awake. The half-bird is truly, fully a clean woman in fatigues, an Olympic athlete driving the now-opaque hummer bull up over the slagheap. "My sister Naomi's death completely changes my life," Ruth says, "I'm going home to settle some scores. I live next to a gun shop. It puts a new spin on family and homelife." The lamb boy Raed soon follows her in a blur of social backgrounds. The scene shifts, slightly deranged, a mammoth plywood construct boxed within a soundproofed room inside an artwork titled "The Lake."

There, on the shore, English-speaking poets digitalized for a red weather roar their winged-lion names across the vast water.

—— **Forwarded Message Follows** ——

From: "Ossama Husein" <STUDENT/OHussein> Organization: Sudan
State University
To: kjohnson@student.highland.cc.il.us
Date: Fri, 28 Aug 1998 13:52:55 -0500
Subject: (Fwd): Khartoum Translation Conference

Dear Mr. David Bromige:

It is to our delightful attention that the poetry of Sudan is now discussed
in the poetry of America with such suddenness. Thank you for being
a section of this and for making a vision of a poet of Sudan. In ways I
believe you do not suspect, you have entered the Arab nation's literature.
It is my principle, nevertheless, that you must be delighted by this.

Please excuse my English, but I am writing to invite you, as a poet
first of Canada and now, secondarily, of America, to what I now wish
to present. I am speaking concerning a conference (International)
devotional to translation in all the sense of this word. We are interested,
with specificness, in the doubled (tripled!) voices passed through many
mediators of history and cultural ignorance. Irony, as I feel you must
conceptualize, is big here. Irony, in its bigness, becomes something
other. It is like, for an example, you, a Sudanese poet speaking through
an English tongue of brokenness. Or it is like many, many things: For an
example, if I may twice say so: It is like two boys kissing in the shadows
of a pharmaceutical plant. (They are like black and deep wells. Their lives
inside are very, very rich.) The sun will come up over this dusty land and
an ancient hatredness shall fill them.

I do not know if I put myself well. So may I directly ask. Will you come
to Khartoum? Please close your heavy eyes and dream of my branching
hand opened out to you.

We passion to invite another poet of America, Mr. Kent, who also is
credenced in your two countries, and perhaps others, to be a racist. (In his
reply to our Central Council, he spoke: "I am honestly not sure.") Still we
are opened, and we have most little, but our flowing tents which appear
(to all purposes and meanings) to be sailboats in the desert, are yours.

Our young are fresh and eager, and they shall press into your soft mouth goat cheese with a hurt and surprised look in their eyes. Also, dark-skinned soldiers with golden and musical watches adorn every minareted corner. Yes, you will find Khartoum strange and hospitality-filled, except, as you realize, inside certain surprising circumstances. But lightning on a human is more likely, so really not to worry.

Ethnography, of course, is also interesting to every one of us and to all peoples. Our flowing tents, if I may say it repeatedly (for I, in an addition, am a poet), appear to be sailboats in the desert. Thus, after the morning session, we will convene in Building 242 for tea, the prayers of all religions, and the making of bombs. No one is to be insulted, not even if they do not know how.

Then we will reconvene, as I have said, and talk concerning Ethnography, including the customs of Christian animists to the south, the abandonment of the people of Darfur by the West, the poignancy of American magazines like Look and Cross Cultural Poetics, and the rituals of Buffalo List of Poets.

Well, I am sorry. The situation is very complicated. But here, as the saying goes, we are. Here also, please, is a poem by a youth named Leonel Rugama whom we have invited too, except sadly he was beheaded long ago, at 20 years, by Green Beret students in the country of Nicaragua:

The Earth Is A Satellite Of The Moon

Apollo 2 cost more than Apollo 1 Apollo 1 cost plenty.

Apollo 3 cost more than Apollo 2 Apollo 2 cost more than Apollo 1 Apollo 1 cost plenty.

Apollo 4 cost more than Apollo 3 Apollo 3 cost more than Apollo 2 Apollo 2 cost more than Apollo 1 Apollo 1 cost plenty.

Apollo 8 cost a whole shit-load of money, but no one minded because the astronauts were Protestant they read the Bible from the moon astounding and delighting every Christian and on their return Pope Paul VI gave them his blessing.

Apollo 9 cost more than all of these put together including Apollo 1 which cost plenty.

The great-grandparents of the people of Acahualinca were less hungry than the grandparents. The great-grandparents died of hunger. The grandparents of the people of Acahualinca were less hungry than the parents. The grandparents died of hunger.

The parents of the people of Acahualinca were less hungry than the children of the people there. The parents died of hunger.

The people of Acahualinca are less hungry than the children of the people there.

The children of the people of Acahualinca, because of hunger, are not born, but they hunger to be born, even just to die of hunger.

Blessed are the poor for they shall inherit the moon.

Well, in realness, I do not know why I give this poem, except that I know you very much like poems. Don't you agree it was translated, without doubtfulness, by someone most self-congratulatory, so angry at his own country, yet blind as Oedipus to the terrorisms of non-white peoples? (Forgive me. I am smoking opium from Afghanistan. It betters my English, which you can tell is getting better as this letter, like a martyr, spills.)

Of course, Mr. David, the trip (including camels) is long, like torture, apparently, in its likeness, and you shall be compelled to gift-forth your own plane-fare. In these days, that can be a dangerous incident. I understand, of course. But we sure hope you will say yes. Will you say yes? The people of Sudan and the Darfur await you. Headphones are to be distributed. You are forever one of us.

Sincerely, (although it is not my true name)

Osama Hussein

Twenty Hinged Propositions
in Search of a Lost Political Poem

In my country, murmured Swann through the hood, the clock is a dog
    for time. Time does not mean to be listened to: humiliating in its
    disguises, heedless of the ocean.

The ocean is the death young men hope for, they who are bruised
    chimeras of the poem. The poem is an urn, between silhouettes.

The silhouettes are serious and dark, Odette, nostalgic for space. Space
    makes a fact of their factitiousness.

Factitiousness is a space for forging the truth. The truth, so to speak, is a
    problem for poets.

Poets are problems for the experts of poetry. The experts of poetry cover
    their flesh with signs and greatly fan themselves with scrolls: they
    are part of the weather, these papyrus odes exalting death.

Death is a sky to the hopeful young man. The young man glares back at
    the sun and arches his spine like a young pine in the wind; in my
    country, Odette, it's blowing a gale up on the mountain.

The mountain is a gin-clear river, according to a sutra in Buddhism; you
    can even see salamanders on the bottom, moving their feathery,
    incarnadine gills. Gills open and close; silhouettes become
    an urn; the river is slow as an old dog: beneath the sky it slowly
    flows, carrying the moon.

The moon is a picture on a house-shaped clock. The clock, it is ringed
    with pictures of nightingales, Swann, and when it's their turn
    they sing their mechanical songs, while the experts of poetry
    emerge from the clock to drink from the urn.

The urn cares not about its own lubricity: mind is a donkey, words are a
    horse; they shall be bridled by the grad student. The grad

student, denizen of the mountain, is heedless she is the odalisque
of the search engine; doleful, in her gunny habiment, she whistles
a tune, gazing on the campion and its tiny corolla.

The corolla has no scale; like the moon, it is a mind to the clouds. The
clouds billow up for hundreds of miles, more power therein
than a million Hiroshimas, and when the experts of poetry wake
with a start, soaked to the ashes of their flesh, the periwinkled
sky gleams like a mosque.

The mosque is a place full of arches to which many people come to pray;
temple of Delight, wherein Veiled Melancholy has her sovran
shrine, it is an urn to the silhouettes: the forger steals the flax
and lays it on the altar of the experts of poetry, who move
their feathery, incarnadine gills deep in the clear water of the
flowing mountain. The mountain slowly flows beneath the
helicoptered sky.

The sky is structured like a language, with machines, wetness, weather,
and phosphorous; it is like clock work: bodies pile up like phrase
hits in the ward. A ward, Odette, is a place to which many people
come to pray.

To pray is what children did at bedtime, in the early 1960s, wearing
pajamas with little helicopters and missiles, rubber soles on
the booties, like those of my brother and me. My brother and me,
like, once we were kneeling there by the bed, and I was five or
six and he was three or four, and I looked over at him beside me
there, his little hands folded and his eyes shut tight, his lips
moving, and I don't know why, but I unfolded my hands and I
lifted one of them up and I slapped him as hard as I could across
his little face as it prayed for all the other children of the world,
and he fell over and started to gasp and weep on the floor, but I
don't remember anything after that, just the gasping and the
weeping.

The gasping and weeping of people inside a sky that is structured like a
        language is very boring in poems, for poems should be abstract
        and should give pleasure. Pleasure is a violence from within that
        protects us from a violence without, said the expert of poetry.

Poetry should not be about, he said, for to be "about is the old taboo."
        The old taboo is a problem for poets: it thrashes about
        impolitely like a grad student on phosphorous fire, clawing up
        the acclivity of the desolate fell; something huge and metallic
        inscribes white signs overhead, annular and abstract, on the sky's
        blue page.

The page is ensorcelled, Swann, torn from its incunabulum. The
        incunabulum was of Modernism, looted from a museum: huge,
        helical skeins of subfusc and papyrus, bound by withe, smolder
        in the deer park.

The deer park is a pleasant place for the practice of Buddhism.
        Buddhism, purporting to counter narcissism, is increasingly
        connected to position-taking with a vengeance in the American
        literary field.

The field is covered in acanthus and ailanthus; deracinated wisteria
        withers in piles along the runway in the New Jersey sun. The
        New Jersey sun is warm in the documentary about the
        Geraldine Dodge Festival; the sound of jet engines and the
        sound of the ocean are edited from the film.

Film viridescently covers the ornamental pond. The pond cools
        symmetrical bundles of long, metallic rods; it is early spring.

Spring is coming earlier, Odette, and getting warmer. Warmer is what
you get, my Swann, when you have a "political poem" in hand, and
you're near the bottom of the donkey, stumbling, with a hood on.

BAGHDAD EXCEEDS ITS OBJECT

I want to be in the class of people who did . . . the thing that met the aesthetic of the
moment.
　　　　　　　—Douglas Feith, Under-Secretary of Defense,
　　　　　　　　　as quoted in *The New Yorker.*

Come off it, Tha'lab, you faker, you *kadhib,*
yes, very funny, but for goodness sake—
just put back those purple bowels in your tummy,
you'll be late for work!

Make haste, Safia, you little scamp, you pig-tailed *qasida,*
put that fat flap of scalp back on your crown—
now's not the hour for teenage pranks,
it's time to go to school!

Ah, quit moaning Miss Al-Sayab, you *muwashshara,*
we know that fetus hanging from your bottom is a rubber trick—
we're not stupid, you know, so cease being crass,
and get ye to market!

Cut the crap, Nizar, you *iltizam,*
pick that torso up and put it back on your dancing spine—
we know that old box and mirror trick,
now get thee to prayers!

Hey, Rashid, you *al-nahda,*
we know you love the special effects of Hollywood movies,
but it's not safe to make yourself into a geyser of fire—
and anyway, you're supposed to be accompanying the inspectors!

Say there, little Samih, you *shirnur,*
six-month-olds aren't supposed to be able to fly—
so get down from those power lines and gather
your legs and head on the ground here, you naughty child!

Listen, Tawfiq, you *tafila*,
OK, so you're a sorry-assed academic with a Ba'ath mustache,
but put your brains back into your head, you can't fool us by calling in
        sick—
it's time for class and your students are ablaze!

Yo bro, my main-man Bashad, you *tardiyyat*,
you're as if dead and white as marble, but there's not a scratch on your
        body—
quit fucking around, the mosque is rubble,
make the siren light flash and spin on your ambulance!

Greetings Ahmad, you *badi-kamriyyat*,
put your face back on and also that water pipe hose thing back into your
        belly—
yeah, boo hoo, so your kid died of dysentery . . .
Suck it up! The price is worth it!
Now pick up that basket of sweet fruits and gum!

Good morning, Mrs. al-Jurjani, you *madin*,
author of four essays on postmodern currents in American poetry,
what are you howling and wailing like that for, hitting your skull
against the flagstones like a mechanical hammer?
A horse is a horse, and if a horse is dead, a horse is dead—
More so, you are naked, which is unbecoming of a lady your age and
        standing.
Like Hamlet, your emotion is unconvincing, for it exceeds its object.
Therefore, we beseech thee: Show some gratitude, and put a plug in it.

Lyric Poetry After Auschwitz, or: "Get the Hood Back On"

. . . [T]he guard force should be actively engaged in setting the conditions for successful exploitation of the internees . . . by MI (Military Intelligence).
  —Maj. General Geoffrey Miller, Commanding officer of U.S. detention
    centers in Iraq, in internal policy recommendation report, August, 2003.

What's up, Ramal, I'm an American boy, a father, two children, graduate of Whitman High, where I was a member of the Science Club and Student Council, then I got to be the youngest elected officer ever in the history of my town's Rotary Chapter, I'm in charge of fund-raising, which hasn't been easy the past few years, what with the economy and all, but we're hanging in there. I hope you won't take this the wrong way, because I don't want to assault your sensibilities, or anything like that, but I want to be up front with you because I believe that honesty is the best policy: So, I'm going to put a pointed plastic hood on your black and blue head, and then I'm going to stand your caped body on a milk box, with live wires taped to your outstretched hands, and then I'm going to count to ten, you witch-like Arab freak, and maybe I'll flip the switch and maybe not, it all kind of depends. By the time you get to MI, you'll be softened up, and you'll tell us where the terrorists are.

Hi there, Hazaj, I'm an American girl, former Vice-President of the Heartland High Young Democrats and Captain of our Regional Championship pom-pom squad, which no one ever expected to even make it to the second round, it was just amazing, we had our pictures in all the papers and stuff, you should see my scrap book. I hope this isn't awkward and uncomfortable for you, and I hope you don't mind my starting out by just getting straight to the point and saying so: But I'm going to fuck you in the ass now with a fluorescent light tube, you sorry-assed, primitive thug. By the time you get to MI, you'll be softened up, and you'll tell us where all the hidden weapons of mass destruction are.

Welcome, Kamil, I'm an American girl, nineteen, pregnant, my Dad is an alcoholic, but my Mother is in recovery, with her own Daycare, and I'll be taking it over after the Army, I've always wanted to have my own business, and I'm going to expand beyond just one location, I'm not thinking small. And since I believe it is always important to say what one means and not beat around the bush, I want you to know something:

I'm going to hold a pistol to your head and tell you to jack-off, while you recite the Koran as fast as you can, you heathen, Hell-bound fuck, and then I'm going to look at the camera with a cigarette dangling from my sultry, teenage lips, giving the thumbs up. By the time you get to MI, you'll be softened up, and you'll tell us where the missing evil Baathists are.

A pleasure to meet you, Khafif, I'm an American boy, former Homecoming King and now Little League coach and Assistant Manager in-training at Wal-Mart, which is providing jobs and low prices for our depressed area, which has been really hard hit ever since Maytag left town, life is tough sometimes. I hope you won't mind my directness, but I strongly believe men should say what they mean, without pulling any punches, so here's the deal: I'm going to shove a fifteen inch dildo down your mouth, while you crawl all over your naked comrades and they crawl all over you, as if you were all a pile of maggots crawling on the rotting body of a dead Imam—don't whimper, motherfucker, or I'll shove the rest of it in, you towel-headed, perverted piece of filth. By the time you get to MI, you'll be softened up, and you'll tell us where the gangster friends of Saddam's demonic sons are.

Nice to meet you, Tawil, I'm a single girl, with an on-line degree in Social Work, a member of the 700 Club and my church choir, and I'm completely against evolution, which goes against the Holy Bible, as you may or may not know, but in the new Iraq you'll get a better chance to know it for sure, and maybe you'll be saved. And because I believe people should always tell the truth to each other, no matter what their race or creed, I'm going to give it to you straight: I'm going to make you suck the cock of your comrade Wafir, until he comes in your mouth and you swallow it, unless you want to get packed in ice like all the other ones at all the other detention centers besides this one, and then I'm going to put a leather collar around your neck, because it's come down the chain of command, a long, long ways, and then I'm going to clip a leather leash onto it, and then I'm going to make you follow me down the long hallway of Abu-Ghraib, squirming like a slug, crying out in falsetto the names of your tent-wearing wife and your babbling, lice-ridden sons. By the time you get to MI, you'll be softened up, and you'll tell us where all the videos and photos of Saddam's torture prisons are . . . We know they are somewhere, hidden in some deep, wet place, you Babylonian, porn-loving fag. And we're going to get what we want and what we need, no matter how deep down we have to dig. Look at the camera when I talk to you, asshole, or I'll go get the dog.

Hi there, Madid, I'm an American poet, twentyish, early to mid-thirtyish, fortyish to seventyish, I've had poems on the *Poets Against the War* website, and in *American Poetry Review* and *Chain*, among other magazines, and I have a blog, and I really dig Arab music, and I read Adorno and Spivak, and I'm really progressive, I voted for Clinton and Gore, even though I know they bombed you a lot, too, sorry about that, and I know I live quite nicely off the fruits of a dying imperium, which include anti-war poetry readings at the Lincoln Center and the Poetry Project, with appetizers and wine and New World Music and lots of pot. And because nothing is simple in this world, and because no one gets out unscathed, I'm going to just be completely candid with you: I'm going to box your ears with two big books of poems, one of them experimental and the other more plain speech-like, both of them hardbound and by leading academic presses, and I'm going to do it until your brain swells to the size of a basketball and you die like the fucking lion for real. You'll never make it to MI because that's the breaks; poetry is hard, and people go up in flames for lack of it everyday. By the time any investigation gets to you, your grandchildren will have been dead over one thousand years, and poetry will be inhabiting regions you can't even begin to imagine. Well, we did our best; sorry we couldn't have done better . . . I want you to take this self-righteous poem, soak it in this bedpan of crude oil, and shove it down your pleading, screaming throat.

Now, get the hood back on.

CPSIA information can be obtained at www.ICGtesting.com
Printed in the USA
LVOW071609251011

252036LV00003B/102/P

9 781905 700950